Jenny Randles is a pro
number of previous boo
conferences in America
der Director of Invest
Scientific Study of Ano

Peter Hough is Chairman of a northwestern team of paranormal researchers based in Manchester. He has published
research articles in a variety of magazines and has taken part
in radio and television documentaries.

By Jenny Randles

JENNY RANDLES
and PETER HOUGH

Death By
Supernatural Causes?

GRAFTON BOOKS

A Division of the Collins Publishing Group

LONDON GLASGOW
TORONTO SYDNEY AUCKLAND

Grafton Books
A Division of the Collins Publishing Group
8 Grafton Street, London W1X 3LA

A Grafton Paperback Original 1988

ISBN 0-586-20147-5

Printed and bound in Great Britain by
Collins, Glasgow

Set in Ehrhardt

Contents

Introduction

There is a longing in all of us to reach out beyond the boundaries of humdrum everyday life and clutch fearfully in the dark at unknown things.

As a breed, we are fascinated and thrilled by accounts of paranormal and supernatural phenomena: Unidentified Flying Objects, the power of psychokinesis, confrontations with non-human entities and apparitions. The popular press pander to this intrinsic need, factual accuracy often being the first casualty in the war over circulation figures.

Books about supernatural 'mysteries' are ten a penny. They fill the bookshops every Christmas time. A minority are well documented works which contribute genuinely towards our knowledge of 'unknown things', but most are compiled by armchair enthusiasts and consist of material cribbed off other writers, who in turn copied from other books and journals. It is rather like the general's message passed along a line of infantry: 'Give the order to advance.' By the time it reaches the captain, the message has become: 'Lend us three and fourpence for a dance.'

Of course you cannot research every single item in a book, otherwise it would be twenty years in the writing, but there is a danger in accepting *everything* at face value, just because it makes a good story.

We wanted to examine certain alleged cases of supernatural and paranormal phenomena to determine if the facts as originally reported were correct. But we decided to target our researches in a very specific way. We did not wish to compile a wishy-washy collection of mystery stories. Instead we concentrated our attentions on those cases which had generated a lot of publicity, where perhaps there had been a death, possible death, or the disappearance of someone under very strange circumstances. There was a very good reason for this decision.

Although it is very interesting to hear that so-and-so saw a 'ghost', it can remain nothing more than an intriguing anecdote. But to hear, as in the case of Zigmund Adamski, examined in Chapter 5, that the body of a missing man has turned up on top of a coal heap in broad daylight, halfway down a hill overlooked by houses, and in sight of a railway station; that is more interesting. Especially when no one can account for the five days missing from the dead man's life, and one of the police officers involved in the case is then, allegedly, abducted and taken aboard a UFO.

To hear of a young Scottish nanny on trial for 'witchcraft' in Italy, accused – so the newspapers and television broadcasts told us – of trying to burn a young child alive using psychic means; that is much more interesting than the case of the man who merely saw a ghost on his way home from work. Why?

Where death or abduction is involved, the state machine crawls into action. There follows, in theory at least, a thorough investigation by police, lawyers, coroners and forensic experts. If these official investigations are carried out objectively and sensibly, then at the end of the day it should be fairly easy to determine if there was a paranormal element as originally reported, or whether it was just the invention of the media with the help of certain self-styled experts. For as Conan Doyle said, in the person of Sherlock Holmes,

'When you have eliminated the impossible, whatever remains, *however improbable*, must be the truth.'

It is a pity this kernel of wisdom is not remembered in our courtrooms.

For those who have lost a husband or daughter under bizarre circumstances, the last thing they may want is a further public airing of their tragedy. In the case of Jacqueline Fitzsimon, described in Chapter 4, we thought very carefully before including it in this book. But we felt her family had been given a raw deal, on the one hand by the authorities and on the other by certain mystery writers.

In the three years since its occurrence, grossly misleading accounts of the incident have appeared in three different books. This is just fodder to the debunkers. We felt we had a duty to present the facts as we found them. After all, we were the only members of the paranormal community who actually investigated the case.

We are not armchair enthusiasts, neither are we journalists out to make a fast buck at the expense of a gullible public (although the money would come in useful). However, we do accept that things occur outside the parameters of orthodox understanding. But as investigators, we treat each case on its merit. Our credentials are honesty and objectivity.

Much of the material in this book has never been published before. Where possible we have consulted source material, and interviewed many of those directly involved in these quite extraordinary cases: witnesses, police officers, newspaper reporters, parapsychologists, television film makers, psychologists and fire officers.

Not all of it was plain sailing. Some interviews never materialized. Occasionally, promising-looking leads became dead ends. Witnesses sometimes exercised their right to remain silent. An entire chapter planned for inclusion never made it at all.

Satanist Derry Mainwaring Knight, who was accused by his ex-lover of butchering three children during black magic rituals, was jailed for seven years on a charge of fraud in 1986. It was claimed he had conned £250,000 out of several wealthy Christians for a phoney crusade against other satanists. The story made front-page headlines.

Knight, overweight and balding, befriended the Reverend

John Baker in 1983 in dire financial and emotional straits. His third wife had just been involved in a serious car smash, and his contracting business was in difficulties. Eventually he confessed to the kindly vicar that he had been inducted into satanism by his grandmother when he was only eight years old. Afterwards, a faceless apparition had appeared in his bedroom and told him he 'was born for destruction'.

He now wanted to fight the satanic cult which had him in its grip, and follow a Christian way of life. To do this, he told the Reverend Baker, he needed money, lots of money, to kit himself out in expensive regalia and 'buy' his way to the top of the organization. Once there, he could destroy it from within.

Baker, with the help of his bishop, acquired £2,500 from a charity, and handed it over to Knight. This was only the beginning. Donations from a number of Christians were handed over amounting to a quarter of a million pounds. Cheques were thrown at him like confetti. Far from using the money to fight satanism, King had the time of his life. He bought a Rolls Royce, financed a high-class prostitution racket, and daubed a bevy of beautiful women with jewellery and expensive clothes.

Amongst those taken in were Michael Warren, a JP and former High Sheriff, Lord Hampden, Lord Brentford, and Susan Sainsbury, the wife of MP Tim Sainsbury.

The media had a field day at the expense of these 'pillars of society' who, it seems, behaved unwisely. But apart from being wealthy, they were intelligent individuals, and one wonders how they could have been taken in by such an obvious conman – if that was all there was to Derry Mainwaring Knight.

We followed the trial with great interest, and some of it did not make sense. We felt there might be more behind the story than was being said in court or printed in the newspapers. Knight claimed to be a 'Grand Archdeacon of

Satanism' and 'High Priest' of a coven which conducted Black Masses in Hockley Wood, Essex. This sounded like something straight out of Dennis Wheatley, but we wanted to know more. This was just the sort of case which cried out for investigation.

It was from her American hideout that Knight's ex-lover Angela Murdock told the press of his claim to have abducted and sacrificed three children. She never saw any evidence of this, but did come across a jar of blood in her refrigerator one day.

There were many questions we wanted answers to. Was there something more than gullibility which drove this exclusive set of people to part with tens of thousands of pounds? Did Knight really butcher three young children, or was his story just schoolboy bravado aimed at impressing and frightening his girlfriend? What, if anything, did the police uncover?

We wanted to research the story from the inside, starting with all the principal players – including Derry Mainwaring Knight – and present the full facts, giving those involved the opportunity to present the Christian viewpoint on satanism.

We approached the Reverend Baker, Lord Brentford, Tim Sainsbury MP, Lord Hampden and Derry Knight, via HM Prison Service. The two lords and the MP were brief and to the point: 'I regret I do not think I will be able to assist you in your search' ... 'I have said all I wish to say on the Mainwaring Knight case at the trial and have had quite enough of it' ... 'My wife would not wish to discuss the case to which you refer ...' Who can blame them? They were made a laughing stock. But we were offering to put the record straight.

The reaction of the Prison Service was a little more mysterious. To contact a prisoner, you must go through an elaborate procedure. A letter is sent to HM Prison Service headquarters in London furnishing as many details as possible about the offender, and the reason for your request. Officials then approach the prisoner, and enquire if he would mind you writing or visiting him. If there are no objections, then contact goes ahead.

We wrote to HM Prison Service enclosing the relevant details. Three weeks later we received the following reply from a Mr Daniel Twite: 'It is regretted that no trace of anyone of the above name can be traced in Prison custody.'

According to Mr Twite, Knight did not exist! We knew we had the correct name because defendants are always charged under their real names in court. In reply, we conveyed our bemusement, and enclosed a copy of a newspaper clipping to prove Knight was not a figment of our imaginations. We requested he look at his records again. Since then we have had absolutely no word from HM Prison Service. After seven weeks of patiently waiting, we sent off a further letter, reiterating what we had already said, and finishing with: 'We must advise you that if we have not received a positive response within ten days, then we must explore the possibility that we are being obstructed from contacting this man. Our first course of action will be to contact our MP.' As we write this, the matter rests in the hands of Lawrence Cunliffe MP.

So far all we have met is a wall of silence. Could there be a cover-up? If so, why? What could Derry Mainwaring Knight tell us that other people would not wish to be aired? Is there a much simpler, straightforward explanation?

If there is, no one is telling us.

The Reverend John Baker was convinced that Derry Mainwaring Knight possessed real satanic powers. While awaiting trial, Baker reportedly made weekly trips to see him in prison. Knight stated in court: 'It was not to discuss the case, but the problems I had with police and other people. Mr Baker endeavoured at all times to try and ensure I did not retaliate through the use of Black Masses against such people.'

We were able to discover that, since the trial, the Reverend Baker has made regular trips to hospital for treatment of leukaemia. We wish him well.

The first part of each section is a dramatization in which we have tried to capture the flavour of the original reports; the second part describes what our own investigations have uncovered.

This book was written with a great deal of enthusiasm. We hope you will read it with equal enthusiasm, and with pleasure.

1

Flight Into Oblivion

The evening was going to be perfect for flying. The Melbourne day had been warm and sunny, with light on-shore breezes bringing the temperature down to the pleasant mid-seventies. Very little cloud spoiled the skies and if there were to be a time to get in some night flying hours, Saturday 21 October 1978 was going to be it.

Frederick Valentich needed those hours. He had almost no solo experience over water. But he loved flying. He had even recently spent two weeks in training at the local Royal Australian Air Force Base. One of the true loves of his life was the Cessna 182 rented from Southern Air Services which he was licensed to pilot, with its callsign letters of VH-DSJ, 'Delta Sierra Juliet'.

That morning over breakfast Guido Valentich, Frederick's father, noticed the excitement in his 20-year-old son's eyes. They sparkled at the prospect of what would be only his second flight alone at night and the first to take him out above the ocean. 'You know how dangerous it can be out there in the dark. There are no landmarks. You can get lost,' Guido cautioned his son. But his words themselves were lost on Frederick. Adrenalin was already pumping through the young flier's veins.

Before leaving for a morning's work Frederick collected $200 from his bedroom. This had been handed to him by officer chums at the Victoria barracks. 'Go collect as many crayfish as you can screw out of those fishermen on King Island,' was his brief. That would call for hard bargaining with the men on the dockside, but it would add spice to his planned adventure.

Frederick Valentich brought something else with him out of his bedroom. It was a rather dog-eared exercise book packed with press cuttings. They were all connected with UFOs, in which he fervently believed. He had studied the works of Eric Von Daniken and Emmanuel Velikovsky and was an ardent fan of the current Steven Spielberg movie, *Close Encounters of the Third Kind*. In this film, which he had seen days before, a group of pilots vanished into space during a flight over water but were returned to earth, looking neither the worse for wear nor a single day older despite thirty years having passed by. Their captors had been child-like, benevolent and ultra-intelligent aliens. Of course, it was a modern myth – a fairy tale. But Valentich knew that the movie represented a deeper reality. Such things could happen. They did happen. He had read about them. 'UFOs exist,' he told his father with assurance. 'During my time with the Air Training Corps at Sale I saw classified material that proved this.'

On that morning, Frederick climbed into his twelve-year-old Fiat to make the journey from Avondale Heights to the army surplus store where he worked on Saturday mornings.

Store owner Dick Williams liked Freddie, yet he did seem to be in a daze that day. Not that this was particularly unusual. His head was very clearly already in the clouds. Freddie's flight would be a 160-mile trip from Moorabbin Field, cutting the coast at Cape Otway and touching down on King Island which was halfway to Tasmania. Theoretically it was a short hop of not much more than an hour, but once above the waters of Bass Strait it would be Valentich, his Cessna and the elements alone. Exactly as he wanted it.

As he left the building sometime after noon Frederick stared at the azure blue sky and said wistfully, 'It's going to be a nice day for flying.' Dick Williams watched him go with a nod. It was to be the last time he would ever see his employee.

The afternoon sun beat down on his car as Frederick drove towards Moorabbin Field. Although he would not depart for King Island until the evening there was something important he had to do there. Valentich was desperate to become a commercial pilot, his one dream after the RAAF turned him down because of poor school grades. He was well on the way towards getting his licence, but still had two courses to complete. One of these, meteorology, would take up three hours' study that afternoon.

Of course, gaining a licence would not guarantee him a job. But Frederick was nothing if not confident of his own abilities. Guido would caution him, 'If you want to fly you should have worked harder at school.' It was not meant unkindly, but perhaps because he sensed the truth of these words, it acted as a source of discomfort to the aviator. But at least he had another opportunity. He was determined not to waste his chance and this time truly make it.

The class ended at about 5 P.M. and now it was time to calculate and file his flight plan for the outbound leg to King Island. It was important to do this conscientiously. Mistakes could come back to haunt him when he had his licence and was in search of a job. He liked to plan his flights like military operations.

By 5.20 P.M. Frederick Valentich was ready. He registered the plan with Moorabbin flight control, estimating a departure time of 5.35 P.M. and arrival on the island at 6.40 P.M. As sunset was due a few minutes after his arrival time this meant that only the final few moments of his journey would be in the gloomy half twilight of a spring evening. If he made a hash of things he could spend the night on King and return in daylight. His options on what to do were in fact wide open. Indeed he did not even call ahead to King and ask them to switch on the runway lights. Whether this was a mistake, a calculated risk or other factors intruded, the die was cast as the flight plan left his hands.

It should now have been time to start the pre-flight checks and prepare for take-off. He had allowed only fifteen minutes for this, just about enough. But instead Frederick Valentich did something rather odd. He went to a nearby McDonald's for a hamburger and did not return to Moorabbin Field until after 6 P.M.

Meanwhile, across the city of Melbourne to the northwest, a 31-year-old man sat over a radar set. Steve Robey was a commercial pilot with ten years' experience but was acting as duty air traffic controller at Tullamarine, the principal airport in the region.

By the standards of Heathrow or John F. Kennedy this was not a difficult job. But it was none the less a demanding one. Robey had to know what traffic was inbound, outbound or merely passing through and ensure that the aircraft kept out of one another's way. The radar was a help in this endeavour, but it had its limitations, owing both to its power and size and to the Otway mountains that loomed to the southwest.

As Steve Robey knew perfectly well, his most important task was to act as a reassuring voice on the ground-based end of the two-way radio. Up there in the sky it can be lonely and frightening, especially if something should go wrong. Calmly and efficiently he must ensure that any nervous pilot became aware that, however bad things might appear in the cockpit, down at Tullamarine things were under control. To Steve Robey, the jaunt by Frederick Valentich across the Bass Strait was no big deal; just one more flight he would have to shepherd that night.

The young pilot finally returned to Delta Sierra Juliet and began to check her over. A hired plane presented some difficulties. It was not usually known who had flown her last or how careful that pilot had been. So Valentich never hurried his examination. He found, as expected, that the tanks were far from full, so he topped them up. Indeed he did so far

beyond his needs. He put in enough fuel to fly to King Island
and back several times over. If he wanted to miss the island
altogether and fly on to Tasmania that would be no problem.

At 6.19 P.M. Frederick Valentich began his take-off and
climbed into a sky already turning indigo across the eastern
horizon. Everything went well as he soared to his initially
cleared height of 1500 feet and began his southward sweep.

Steve Robey cut in on the radio. 'We copy your take-off
. . . Delta Sierra Juliet . . . Have a good flight . . . We'll expect
a call when you reach the Cape.'

The Cape was Cape Otway, the marker point with its
lighthouse where Valentich would say goodbye to the safety
of the Victoria mainland. It was ninety-seven miles, easily in
reach in about forty minutes if he followed the line of the
coastal road with the Otway range silhouetted as a backdrop
against the encroachment of the night.

Down on the ground people saw him. But his lights were
only those of one more plane braving the dark. Hardly
anything unusual. Even the fishing boats in the bay hardly
gave a glance as his engine hummed by. They had more
important things on their minds.

By now he was fading from Steve Robey's radar. But this
was both expected and of no concern to the controller.
Around the Cape there was emergency military radar back-
up. The cover-free zone out over the sea was small and
relatively hazardless. There was no real danger expected,
provided Valentich was sensible. With under 200 hours'
flying time the pilot was hardly Charles Lindbergh, but he
should be able to cope with a routine flight.

At 6.53 P.M., as the Cessna neared Cape Otway, Robey
intruded on the private thoughts of Frederick Valentich.
'Delta Sierra Juliet . . . would you like to extend your SAR
time?' The question puzzled the flier until he realized that
his late departure had cut badly into his Search and Rescue
(SAR) time estimate. Every pilot had to give this as an

estimate of when his arrival would be overdue so the authorities would know when to start worrying. There was leeway,
of course. One could always be delayed. But taking off almost
three-quarters of an hour later than planned made his 7.30
P.M. SAR estimate almost meaningless now. He would
probably arrive just before that. But there was no point in
cutting it fine and having the navy on the lookout because he
had mistimed his crossing of the Bass Strait by just a few
minutes.

Valentich acknowledged Robey with what seemed to be
agreement, and then continued his flight in silence. This was
broken just after 7 P.M. when he announced, 'Melbourne,
Delta Sierra Juliet . . . At Cape Otway, descending for King
Island.'

From this point onward Frederick Valentich was truly
alone. He was at 4500 feet and well below radar coverage
from Melbourne, which needs aircraft to be flying at several
thousand feet above this to be detectable.

The calm of the night was suddenly ended at 7.06 P.M.
when Valentich radioed through to Melbourne. His voice was
not strained. It was perfectly normal. 'Ah, Melbourne, this is
Delta Sierra Juliet. Is there any known traffic below five
thousand?'

Steve Robey was momentarily puzzled. He checked his
log. Nothing should be there. 'Delta Sierra Juliet, negative.
No known traffic,' he replied.

The calm voice of the young pilot returned to explain
himself. 'Delta Sierra Juliet, ah, I . . . em . . . seems to be a
large aircraft below five thousand.'

This was sufficient for Robey to immediately put requests
in for a radar sweep of the area. He wanted to know if anyone
could see the Cessna and this unknown aircraft which
definitely, so far as he knew, ought not to be present. If it
was, then it posed a threat to Valentich and upset the
equilibrium of this otherwise ordinary day. Robey decided to

keep the pilot talking. 'Delta Sierra Juliet, what type of aircraft is it?'

'Delta Sierra Juliet, ah . . . I cannot affirm . . . It has four bright, seems to me like landing lights.'

Robey acknowledged the message and waited for data on the radar checks. A minute later the pilot was back with more alarming news. 'Melbourne, this is Delta Sierra Juliet, the aircraft has just passed over me . . . about a thousand feet above.'

'Delta Sierra Juliet, Roger, and it is a large aircraft – confirm?'

'Ah . . . unknown, due to speed of its travelling . . . Is there any air force aircraft in the vicinity?'

By now Robey knew the truth. There were supposedly no aircraft other than the Cessna in the vicinity. So what was Valentich seeing? He told the pilot exactly what the situation was. Valentich remained silent.

Seconds drifted by on the night air. 'Ah, Melbourne,' Valentich came in, 'it's approaching me now from due east . . . towards me.'

The controller acknowledged but was uncertain what to say. He had noticed that the pilot did not seem distressed. He was keeping his nerve remarkably well.

After a pause when the microphone opened and then closed again, Valentich decided exactly what he wanted to add. 'Delta Sierra Juliet . . . ah . . . It seems to me that he's playing some sort of game. He's . . . ah . . . flying over me two . . . three times at speeds I could not identify.'

Steve Robey decided that in these circumstances he should try to retain as much normality as he could so he spent some moments verifying the flight level of the Cessna, which was still 4500 feet. Then he got Valentich to confirm that he was still unable to identify the aircraft. This was a new situation for the ground controller. 'Ah, Delta Sierra Juliet, Roger, standby,' he said.

Ten seconds later Valentich returned with the first hint of strain in his voice. 'Melbourne . . . Delta Sierra Juliet . . . It's not an aircraft . . . It is . . .' The words trailed off into the night.

Robey grabbed hold of the microphone. 'Delta Sierra Juliet, Melbourne. Can you describe the, ah, aircraft?'

The pilot's measured voice did so. Again there seemed a peculiar lack of emotion. It did not seem as if he were worried about the encounter. 'Ah . . . as it's flying past me it's a long shape. I, ah, cannot identify more than that . . . such speed.' Steve Robey was wearing a puzzled frown when Valentich added, 'It's before me right now, Melbourne.'

'Delta Sierra Juliet, Roger. Ah, and how large would the, er, object be?'

As the controller expected, the pilot, despite his aerial proximity to this unknown intruder, was as calm in his reply as before. Following the callsign he launched into a description. 'Melbourne . . . it seems like it's, ah, stationary . . . What I'm doing right now is orbiting and the thing is just orbiting on top of me also. It's got a green light and a sort of metallic like . . . it's all shiny on the outside.'

Steve Robey was by this point becoming concerned. He had no evidence that any strange aircraft should be up with the Cessna, and if it were there, why was it behaving in such a peculiar and potentially hazardous manner? Could it be that Valentich had somehow flipped? Was he seeing things? Was he mistaking ground lights? Whatever the truth the situation could very quickly get out of hand and all he could do for the moment was reply as calmly as possibly and hope the problem rectified itself.

'Delta Sierra Juliet . . .' Valentich called. There were several seconds of silence. 'Ah, it just vanished.'

Robey acknowledged.

'Ah, Melbourne . . . would you know what kind of aircraft I've got? Is it a military aircraft?'

Steve Robey had no reason to think so. But it was possible. An unauthorized mission. A foreign spy plane, even. These had to be options. 'Delta Sierra Juliet ... confirm the, er, aircraft just vanished?'

'Say again?' Valentich appeared preoccupied. He did not give his callsign.

'Delta Sierra Juliet, is the aircraft still with you?'

The pilot began slowly, then cut himself off midstream: 'Delta Sierra Juliet, its, ah, nor ...' He appeared to be about to say 'north'. But if Valentich *was* flying south over the Bass Strait, as he was supposed to be, he ought not to be able to see anything to the north (i.e. behind him). Robey did not realize this immediately. Valentich corrected himself within seconds: '... Now approaching from the southwest.'

Half a minute passed by. It was now almost 7.12 P.M. and approximately six minutes of this cat and mouse game had ensued. Robey had begun an alert status as soon as it was confirmed that the object Valentich was supposedly seeing ought not to be there. This was really all he could do at this stage. But fate was about to take a hand. The young airman came over the radio thirty seconds later with devastating news. 'Delta Sierra Juliet. The engine is rough idling. I've got it set at 23 ... 24 ... and the thing is coughing ...'

Immediately aware of how serious this could be for a single-engined plane alone over water, even without its mysterious attendant, Steve Robey enquired, 'Delta Sierra Juliet, Roger. What are your intentions?'

Again there was no callsign and Valentich did now begin to sound as if he really were in danger. 'My intentions are, ah, to go to King Island. Ah, Melbourne ... that strange aircraft is hovering on top of me again.'

Oh God, Robey thought to himself. What is happening? He had no time to even suggest a course of action.

Valentich, clearly in awe, said, 'It *is* hovering and its *not* an aircraft.' The words 'is' and 'not', very clearly emphasized, were almost the first hints of real emotion.

Robey affirmed. What on earth could hover in station above an aircraft and also perform manoeuvres around it? A Harrier jet?

Six seconds later, at 7.12:28 P.M., Frederick Valentich pressed his microphone switch, apparently for the very last time. 'Delta Sierra Juliet, Melbourne,' he said. This was incorrect radio procedure. He had spoken as if he were ground control, reversing the order of his words. But he added no more. The microphone remained open for seven-teen seconds, during the first twelve of which weird sounds – like metal scrapings or tappings – came over the airwaves. Then followed the hiss of a pressed switch without any words. Then nothing.

Frederick Valentich had said his final words.

Steve Robey tried to establish contact, shouting, 'Delta Sierra Juliet, Melbourne,' into his radio. There was no reply. Almost immediately he upgraded the alert into a general distress call and set any traffic in the area on to the lookout.

At 7.28 P.M. VH-DSJ did not land at King Island. Although Robey had extended the SAR time by half an hour to 8 P.M. an immediate search and rescue mission was launched. In the pitch dark this was not easy. A single light plane retraced the route of the Cessna 182, finding nothing. Anything more substantial had to wait for the dawn of a clear, bright Sunday morning.

A Lockheed Orion of the RAAF Maritime Reconnaissance squadron spent that entire day crisscrossing the area. Flight Lieutenant Bill Sigston did find an oil slick eighteen miles north of King Island. This seemed too far south and appeared too large to come from a small plane, but he dropped a marker beacon and directed a ship to collect samples. These were later analysed at a Maribyrnong laboratory of the

Australian Defence Command. In their view it was from a ship and was not aviation fuel.

Back in Avondale Heights Guido Valentich spent the last worry-free night of his life. Freddie had not returned for a family gathering by 10 P.M. as he had promised. But his father naturally assumed he must have decided to stay overnight on King Island. Perhaps he was waiting for some better crayfish.

But then the Sunday morning radio news carried a report of a lost plane between Victoria and King Island, amidst other stories of UFOs sighted all over the region. The pang of distress turned into horror when Guido called the authorities and learnt the awful truth.

Almost immediately the phone calls began, the newsmen digging for their exclusive stories. How did Guido feel? Did he think that his son was still alive? Where did he believe the UFO had come from – and had it taken Frederick back home with it, wherever home might be?

UFO – what UFO? Guido enquired. And he learnt the full story of his son's bizarre disappearance. He had vanished into oblivion whilst being pursued by a flying saucer!

The calls came from all over the world. By Monday morning it was a nine-day wonder headline on TV and the front pages of newspapers everywhere. Each reporter had a theory. None of them knew the truth. And soon they were no longer interested. The saga brought forth no new evidence. The story went as cold as the ocean in which Frederick could never have lasted more than a few minutes. It was no longer newsworthy and was succeeded by some other topical item.

On Wednesday 25 October 1978, the Orion search plane was called to new duties. It had not found any trace of the Cessna. The other light planes that kept a lookout and the ship crews that maintained a seascape vigil gradually gave up as the story disappeared from the public eye.

The case of VH-DSJ and the mysterious disappearance of

its young and perhaps foolish pilot was now just a part of history, strange but unexplained. However, for Guido Valentich the tragedy would never be over. He had entered a nightmare of doubt and uncertainty – and that nightmare seemed to go on for ever.

INVESTIGATION

The mysterious disappearance of Frederick Valentich created a sensation throughout the Australian continent. But by Monday 23 October 1978 newspaper headlines and TV news stations around the world were featuring this strangest of all 'UFO abductions'.

Even the staid aviation journal, *Flight International*, which avoids UFOs like the plague, carried a brief item, 'Cessna downed by UFO?' in its 4 November 1978 issue. This short account of the facts was very open-minded and free from the usual anti-UFO hysteria that the 'respectable' press tend to present.

Why did the 'UFO abduction' scenario gain such prominence? One key reason had to be that this is what an initial reading of the events appears to indicate. Valentich saw an object that should not have been in the sky, a flying object which he could not identify, and which from his description did not seem to be any standard form of aircraft. The object took evident interest in the Cessna and, following weird metallic noises and a final distressed call from the pilot, neither he nor his aircraft were ever seen or heard from again. That does imply, to some minds in need of mystery, that he was spirited away off the earth by whoever was at the controls of the UFO.

Another reason was that previous incidents had occurred where UFOs had allegedly been responsible for deaths. In May 1983, for example, two youths died beneath the wheels of a freight train on the Liverpool-Manchester line near the town of Huyton. It was 4 A.M. Police enquiries revealed that they had left their motorcycles on the road, for no obvious reason, and fled right into the path of the swift moving diesel. This sad incident seems baffling. But a report was simultaneously received of a UFO sighted in the sky over the exact same part of Merseyside where the boys died and at precisely the same time in the morning. A CID officer on the Merseyside force some months later said that the suggestion that the boys had seen the UFO and been run over by the train as they ran for help or to get other witnesses was as feasible as any other they had to go on.

Australian researcher Paul Norman reports on a similar event at Bourks Flat, Victoria, in the same part of the country where the Valentich mystery unfolded. Nineteen-year-old Gary Taylor died on 7 April 1966 when his car hit a tree. Three days earlier, at that exact spot, a very strange close encounter had taken place when a car driven by Ron Sullivan had met a UFO and had its headlight beams bent by some unexplained force.

But probably the most directly relevant 'UFO death' is that which befell pilot Thomas Mantell over Godman Field, Kentucky, USA on the bright afternoon of 7 January 1948.

The case is too well known to require description (many books have recounted it – for the most current see *The UFO Conspiracy* by Jenny Randles, Javelin, 1988).

Briefly, Mantell piloted his F-51 towards a mysterious target which was also observed from the ground. He climbed well above his safe height ceiling and the wreckage of the plane and his mutilated body were discovered soon afterwards. There is little doubt why he crashed. Lack of oxygen at altitude produced unconsciousness, following which the plane entered a fatal dive and disintegrated. What does remain uncertain is the identity of the object he was chasing (which nobody saw again).

Stories and rumours soon circulated about an alien spaceship that might have 'zapped' Mantell. The authorities, desperate for an answer, invented an implausible one that involved him seeing the planet Venus. This was almost impossible in the middle of the day, and absurd given the vivid description of a 'large, metallic object' that the pilot reported to ground control. However, it temporarily got the US Air Force off the hook (and secret reports, subsequently released, indicate they tried this subterfuge because they privately felt the UFO *had* been a spaceship).

Today, whilst the Mantell story lives on in mythology, most serious researchers believe that the object could have been a research project's Sky Hook balloon. The evidence does remain fairly slim, but what Mantell and the ground observers saw fits the known dimensions of such a huge metallic object.

These cases show how the use of the UFO explanation is both reasonable (because it *has* happened before) and also remarkably popular. People love to speculate about something as mysterious as that.

Of course, in all three cases just described there was no question about the cause of death. The bodies were found in every instance and the autopsies showed the quite natural reasons for the victims' tragic ends. In Valentich's case the body (if indeed there was a body) was never found.

The Victoria UFO Research Society also revealed another factor in the Valentich/UFO equation. His disappearance came amidst a UFO wave. In a paper presented to the MUFON (Mutual UFO Network) annual conference in 1984, Paul Norman told the audience of American UFO researchers that 'over fifty reported observations in that area which occurred before, during and after' the Bass Strait disaster had been logged.

One interesting sighting was at Currie, on King Island itself. This came at 2 P.M. on the day of the Cessna's last flight and involved a single strange cloud in the sky out of which emerged a golf-ball shaped object about one quarter the size of the full moon. It went out over the sea, then returned inland to the mysterious, still stationary cloud.

A cloud also featured in what is perhaps the most intriguing claim of all. Roy Manifold, a plumber, was on holiday near Cape Otway on 21 October 1978. It was 6.45 P.M. and Valentich was then approaching the area in his light plane. Manifold had set up a 35-mm camera on a tripod to photograph the sunset over the Bass Strait. He took six pictures, exactly twenty seconds apart, and saw nothing unusual himself. But when developed, *after* news of the Valentich disappearance broke, pictures 4 and 6 (but *not* number 5, despite it showing the exact same area of sea, sky and sunset) contained anomalies.

Number 4 has what could be interpreted as a 'lump' causing a disturbance in the sea. Number 6 shows an object in the sky above this area of water with a trail or cloud. Neither are very clear or especially solid looking and are almost impossible to reproduce clearly.

Immediate suspicions of film defects were allegedly ruled out by Kodak when they examined the pictures. But it is odd that the above account of the sequence of pictures differs from that given by Ground Saucer Watch (an American team that specializes in subjecting UFO photographs to sophisticated computer enhancement techniques). In their report they say that pictures 5 and 6 are the suspect frames. This anomaly has itself not been clarified to our understanding.

Ground Saucer Watch obtained the pictures by way of Paul Norman, who is quite a globetrotter and visits the USA regularly. In their report they state: 'The first impression one is left with upon viewing the film is that the (image) is an emulsion defect. However, a close examination of the original negatives revealed that the image was not caused by any artifact on the emulsion.' They then rule out 'any known type of cloud or weather phenomena' and say that 'digital densitometry' (one of their techniques for accurately gauging

shadings and shadows) provided evidence of the object being
'of a metallic structure'. Furthermore, they conclude, the
image is blurred by motion and is back-lit by the sun – clearly
pointing to a real structured object about 20 feet in diameter.

William Spaulding of the Ground Saucer Watch team
added, 'It is the consensus of the GSW technicians that the
images represent a bona fide unknown flying object of
moderate dimensions apparently surrounded by a cloud-like
vapor/exhaust residue.'

One man who disagrees is Dr Richard Haines, a NASA
research scientist from California. His qualifications are
extraordinarily impressive. He is a member of the Human
Factors committee of the Aerospace Medical Association,
and a member of the international society of Air Safety
Investigators and a specialist in optics. His interest in UFOs
is proven by his ongoing experiments into witness perception
in UFO cases. His involvement with the Valentich case has
been extensive.

Haines argues that given the conditions the large cloud-like
mass should have been reflected on the sea. It was not. And he
has calculated the optics and finds it inexplicable that Manifold
did not see the UFO if it was really present. He concludes, in
his report on the photographs, 'The dark cloud-like image of
frame 6 was somehow added after the exposure was made at
Cape Otway.' In other words, he says, it was not real.

Given that the UFO evidence surrounding the so-called
Bass Strait flap is rather contradictory and inconclusive, we
are left doubting whether it has anything to do with the pilot's
disappearance.

Of course, it may be relevant in another way. Valentich
would certainly have been aware of some of the recent UFO
activity. His background in ufology has already been shown.
And we have the curious decision of his to take the UFO
scrapbook with him on the flight. This has led some people

to speculate that the pilot may have tried to perpetrate a hoax himself.

It is true that nobody else actually saw the object Valentich claimed he saw. This is not too surprising as it was supposedly well out to sea. But it is a factor to bear in mind. Some journalists seriously offered the controversial Manifold photographs as evidence that the Cessna had exploded. The image on the photographs, it was said, was the disintegrating plane, and the cause of the explosion was some kind of strange energy discharge from a cloud. The main problem with this theory is that the time of the photographs is certain because of the location of the sun in them. So if they did chance to capture the freak destruction of Delta Sierra Juliet we have an even greater supernatural mystery: how Frederick Valentich succeeded in communicating from a disembodied state and a non-existent aircraft nearly half an hour after it had blown up! The final message to Melbourne ground control was quite certainly timed after these photographs were taken.

Guido Valentich wanted to believe in the UFO theory, because it was one of the few circumstances which gave any real hope for the survival of his son. He told the *Melbourne Sun* on 24 October 1978 that he felt Frederick had been 'borrowed' by aliens from another world and was safe and well somewhere. It is understandable, given the encouragement of UFO enthusiasts eager to venture one daft idea after another, that Guido should clutch at this kind of straw. Apparently he received many phone calls from 'well-wishers' determined to convince him of the reality of Venusians, Martians and all brands of friendly 'space people'.

If Frederick Valentich did set up a hoax, what went wrong? Presumably all he wanted to do was become famous (something he certainly achieved) and live to savour the glory (which is far less certain). Was his unfamiliarity with night flying his undoing? Perhaps by concentrating so much on getting his UFO story right and making it convincing for controller Steve Robey he somehow lost command of the aircraft and ditched it into the cold, unforgiving waters of the ocean.

But why did the search turn up no evidence that the plane had crashed? There were a few claims that it did. On 21 November 1978 at 12.31 P.M. a pilot from the Hawk Flying Service thought he saw the outline of an object below the surface of the water forty-eight miles north of King Island. This would coincide perfectly with the last known position of Delta Sierra Juliet, based on the radio transmissions.

Unhappily the pilot lost the wreckage as he circled the area and despite directing other people to look out for it nobody else has ever seen it there. Aviation authorities were extremely sceptical and believed that the pilot had merely mistaken swell for an aircraft outline, largely because the sea bottom is 180 feet deep at this point and it would be almost impossible to view anything at such a depth from the air.

These negative results led to all kinds of ludicrous associations of the area with the mythical Bermuda Triangle (for example a book by journalists Kevin Killey and Gary Lester which turned the Bass Strait into *The Devil's Meridian*). But the seas everywhere have a tendency to keep their dead. Any floating pieces of wreckage would have soon drifted away. Most of the plane would have gone to the bottom. If the aircraft did crash, given the fact that no real visual search was possible for twelve hours afterwards it is not really astonishing that nothing was found.

Ken Williams, assistant director of public relations for the Australian Department of Transport, was nominated to field the enquiries on this case during those hectic first few weeks. He made his personal views clear in a written statement. 'My opinion is that the inexperienced pilot become disorientated and that that disorientation, coupled with Venus, cockpit light reflections and flashing lighthouses, Cape Otway behind and

King Island ahead, created in his mind an illusion that he was being accompanied by a UFO ... He then lost altitude and crashed into the water, possibly in a steep turn.'

So now we have a new suggestion: that Valentich's sighting of the UFO was really an honest mistake, possibly stimulated by his known belief in the subject. It was even speculated by some (who knew little of aviation) that the UFO was really the lights of Delta Sierra Juliet which Valentich, in his inexperience, had inverted. Flying upside down, these reflected on the water and seemed to the pilot to be in the air. This is totally untenable, if only because the Cessna would not have been able to fly like this for more than a few seconds without crashing and the tapes of the air to ground transmissions suggest the UFO, whatever it was, was visible far longer than that.

Another clue which surfaced during the protracted enquiries into this case concerned the apparent lack of emotion shown by Valentich during the crisis. Controller Steve Robey was interviewed by the *Melbourne Herald*, which resurrected the case on 9 December 1980. He said: 'Towards the end I think [Valentich] was definitely concerned for his safety; I considered that he would have to be a good actor to have put it all together the way he did ... It sounded as though it was rattling him ... he was a little mixed up.'

Others, such as Dr Richard Haines, do not entirely agree. Haines is one of the few researchers to have heard the official tape recording of the communications (never made public, although a transcript was). He feels that mostly the pilot is remarkably calm and restrained. Indeed he speculates about the possibility that Valentich is reading a script which he has prepared in advance to create the UFO hoax.

This might support another theory that was suggested early on; that Valentich had engineered his own disappearance in a kind of sophisticated fake suicide. Some of the reasons for this suspicion are based on mistaken assumptions made by the media. The fact that neither the Cessna nor the UFO were detectable by ground radar produced the speculation that the UFO did not exist and Delta Sierra Juliet was not in the position Valentich claimed it was in. In truth the limitations of the radar system would almost certainly have made both UFO and aircraft undetectable if the heights given were correct.

On the other hand some things do support this hypothesis. Valentich did file a one-way flight plan. That itself is not too unusual, but odd when coupled with the amount of fuel put into the Cessna: far in excess of what was required even for a return trip to King Island. Ken Williams of the Department of Transport says that Valentich could have flown for five hours or almost 700 miles, instead of the 160-mile journey planned. Did he perhaps always intend to continue on to another destination (e.g. Tasmania), using the UFO 'abduction' as a convenient smokescreen?

Most of these theories were evaluated by the Department of Aviation during their lengthy investigation of the incident. The report (Reference V116/783/1047) was published in May 1982 and given only a very limited circulation 'to parties having a bona fide interest in the occurrence'. It concludes 'not known' about the location and time of the incident and adds, 'The reason for the disappearance of the aircraft has not been determined.'

Bill Chalker, an industrial chemist widely considered to be Australia's leading UFO investigator, succeeded in obtaining direct access to the Royal Australian Air Force files on UFOs in 1982. This access was officially sanctioned and was unrestricted. They contained nothing on the Valentich disappearance, and the reason cited when Chalker enquired was that the Department of Aviation had not asked the RAAF to investigate.

When Chalker was later given access to the Department of Aviation UFO files he was denied all those which referred to the Valentich case on the grounds that it was an air accident rather than a UFO incident. However, Bill Chalker did succeed in discussing the case at some length with Mr A. Woodward, the man who signed the May 1982 report on the incident. He would not be drawn on UFOs, and preferred to dwell on the many possible natural explanations, but admitted that nobody really knew what had happened.

Bill Chalker takes a particular delight in some of the wilder stories that have circulated about the case. These began quietly enough with the idea that Delta Sierra Juliet might have seen a balloon being used by smugglers to ferry drugs and crashed after colliding with the guide ropes trailing down into the water. Below, the drug smugglers were presumably sailing merrily along, secure in the knowledge that if the coastguard should arrive they need only release the balloon.

Then there is the tale of the mercenary deep-sea divers. This emerged when film producer Ron Cameron was planning a documentary on the Valentich case in late 1982. Two divers approached him claiming that during a routine salvage search for a boat they had found the blue and white Cessna, Delta Sierra Juliet. It was amidst a formation of light planes, all mysteriously lying on the sea bed off Cape Otway, lined up in close proximity to one another!

These suspect characters wanted $10,000 in exchange for photographs and directions to the exact position on the sea bed. Needless to say Cameron was hardly going to fall for that, although he attempted to keep negotiations open when they showed some photographs that did appear to depict a Cessna with the correct registration letters. Apart from a bend in the middle it seemed relatively intact. The divers claimed there was no body inside.

Guido Valentich was very concerned by all this. He told the *Sydney Sun* on 11 January 1983 that it was disappointing that these men 'haven't got the dignity or courtesy to come along and show [the photographs] to me'. When the Department of Aviation made clear that they would have to be involved in any salvage operation and Cameron began to display inevitable doubts about the veracity of this wild story the divers backed off and disappeared from sight.

As Bill Chalker said in a December 1984 report to the magazine *Flying Saucer Review*, 'It is unfortunate that such a situation imposes still further hardships on the Valentich family. If it is within the power of anyone to solve the mystery, surely they must be morally obliged to do so.'

Another fairly predictable development was the appearance of psychics claiming to have news of the missing pilot. Colin Amery from New Zealand claims he has communicated with Valentich during an 'extraterrestrial seance', when the young man explained how he was living on a planet circling a star in the Ursa Major constellation. The aliens had taken him there because they needed his skills . . . although exactly what those skills might be, Amery did not specify.

Guido Valentich, whilst sceptical, is willing to listen to anyone who might help. Unfortunately, other mediums have placed his son in the hands of assorted alien groups and, in at least one case, under the Tasman Sea in a 'hollow-earth colony'. Consistency is not their forte.

Just two months after the Valentich story broke another major event occurred above Kaikoura, New Zealand. A Safe-air Argosy cargo plane, piloted by John Randle, observed some strange lights. They were also tracked on radar by ground control at Wellington. Because of the interest in UFOs created by the disappearance of the Cessna, an Australian TV company asked one of their reporters, Quentin Fogarty, who was vacationing in New Zealand, to film an item for them. Gathering a film and sound crew of husband and wife team David and Ngaire Crockett he went one better and persuaded Safe-air to let them ride the same route in their other Argosy, piloted this time by Bill Startup.

They flew on the night of 30/31 December 1978 and

planned merely to get an atmospheric sequence showing the scenery at night as witnessed days earlier by Captain Randle. Instead, as the world soon discovered, more UFOs were seen over Kaikoura and appeared on several minutes of colour TV film which was sold to networks all around the globe (including the BBC in Britain who gave it lead item treatment on the news).

The story is a complex one, best studied through the book by Bill Startup and co-pilot Bob Guard, *The Kaikoura UFOs* (Hodder and Stoughton, 1981). It was widely panned by critics and the film shows little but dancing lights. Nevertheless, Jenny Randles has corresponded at some length with John Cordy, a former air traffic controller at Heathrow, who looked after the radar at Wellington on the night of the first encounters. He is convinced that something quite extraordinary did happen.

TV journalist Quentin Fogarty produced his own book on the saga, published by Angus and Robertson in 1982 with the title *Let's Hope They're Friendly*, based on words spoken during his live TV commentary aboard the aircraft. In this he reports on a somewhat off-centre investigation into the aftermath of the Valentich case which he undertook.

Fogarty persuaded Guido Valentich to send some of Frederick's personal effects to an American psychic called Pat Gagliardo. She practises psychometry, which involves getting 'impressions' from objects by holding them. In this case she was convinced that Valentich had landed safely and camouflaged his plane, probably in Tasmania. So impressed was Fogarty (and he claimed that leading American UFO researcher, astronomer Dr J. Allen Hynek, endorsed Mrs Gagliardo) that the journalist flew to America to continue the study.

In these second sessions the psychic gave precise descriptions of a place in northwest Tasmania which Fogarty (no doubt at someone else's expense) promptly flew to. He was amazed at how well the psychometrist had described the area where Valentich for some reason had supposedly gone to live a new life. However, nobody there knew anything about it and no one had discovered a Cessna in the bush (it not being easy to see how you could permanently hide a plane).

Whilst compiling the account for this book Jenny Randles met both Dr Richard Haines and Bill Chalker.

Dr Haines had for some time been struggling to complete a mammoth report on his investigation into the disappearance. The report, entitled *Melbourne Incident*, was privately published and turned out to be rather unusual. Haines had created four fictionalized dramas of what might have happened, three of them centred on the main theories: UFO abduction, disorientation and crash, and self-engineered disappearance. This was an odd way of presenting the facts and it sometimes led to considerable confusion as to what was known to be true and what was merely being supposed.

But it was Dr Haines's fourth theory that was most intriguing, as it was original. He suggested that the Americans, who have a military research facility at Pine Gap, near the Bass Strait area, might have been engaged in covert 'star wars' weaponry testing using high-power lasers which would create startling effects in the sky and lead to the many UFO sightings in the area. His fictional drama has Valentich being commissioned (in top secret) to go on behalf of the Australian government to observe the results of the testing from the air. Since they did not want to upset the Americans, this use of a civilian pilot was considered preferable to despatching a RAAF jet. Unfortunately, so Dr Haines guesses, the weapons test, as a sort of forerunner of systems designed to shoot down military satellites, went wrong. The Cessna was immobilized with fatal consequences. Everyone who knew the truth then became subject to a massive cover-up.

This idea is really quite ingenious. One even wonders if Dr Haines' background gives him a little inside knowledge which he is juggling with to tell this story. But it makes an awful lot of assumptions, not least being the possibility of such advanced weapons tests as far back as 1978, and the likelihood of these being conducted not only above a foreign country, but away from the vast desert outback available. Victoria is one of the few parts of Australia where the Americans could virtually guarantee to be spotted.

However, one of the most important things which Dr Haines has done is analyse the strange metallic noises heard during the final part of the radio transmissions from Delta Sierra Juliet. A very complex report has resulted. Its most important conclusions are about what the sounds are *not*.

They are not, it would seem, the microphone switch being keyed quickly, or any attempt to produce a morse code message. There is also no voice content at all. The sounds come in two bursts, one ten seconds long and the other four seconds. There is a gap between them of just under a second when there is no sound at all. Haines speculates about this possibly resulting from the tape recording having been edited. There has always been a school of thought which said that the released version of the tape (heard by very few people – even Guido had considerable problems getting access to it) is censored in some way, perhaps because the pilot said things which the authorities would prefer that nobody hear. As is so often the case in this perplexing story, we are left guessing and speculating.

Bill Chalker is an extremely sensible and responsible investigator. He clearly had done his best to fathom out this mystery, but was reluctant to be drawn into any kind of speculation. 'This is a strange case,' he told Jenny Randles. 'Any number of possibilities might apply.' A suspicion that he favoured the prospect of Valentich creating a hoax (and either crashing or purposely disappearing) was hinted at. But Chalker was happy to consider other options and was giving the Richard Haines 'secret weapons test' the time of day. But he was not persuaded that sufficient hard evidence had been found by the scientist for his proposition. 'I want to study his report more carefully first,' Chalker said with typical restraint.

Bill Chalker ventured to suggest one other fascinating theory, allegedly shared with him by a Department of Aviation official who seemed to take it seriously. 'It was suggested,' Chalker said, 'that Delta Sierra Juliet was struck by a piece of space debris or a meteorite. It would be a fantastic chance, but it just could happen.' Its major drawback is relating it to the rather long duration of the UFO sighting which is suggested by the radio transmissions. But the idea does account for the sudden demise of the plane and almost total destruction of all wreckage.

Maybe so, but as Bill Chalker so rightly summarized, we will possibly never learn the truth for certain: 'It is all a matter of conjecture and speculation. Nobody really knows what happened, and unless someone finds the wreckage, or Valentich turns up one day, probably nobody ever will.'

2
The Charge is Attempted Murder – by Witchcraft!

Carol Compton was barely out of her teens. She was a very pretty girl, with long dark hair and a fresh complexion. Carol was born on Christmas Eve in Aberdeen, the granite city, in the shadow of the Grampian Mountains. Little could she have realized that she would see her twenty-first birthday dawn through the bars of a prison cell in a foreign land.

Like a lot of children today, Carol was the victim of a broken home. Starved of affection as a child, this young woman spent much of her leisure time reading romantic fantasy: the Mills and Boon Kid.

In the winter of 1982 Carol finally met the man of her dreams. He was Italian, and worked as a waiter at the Turnberry Hotel. Carol fell deeply in love, and Marco Vitulano became very fond of the girl with the beautiful eyes and gentle voice.

Carol was intoxicated. She had made her mind up. Marco was her man. She saw wedding bells and several wee bairns around her feet. But although Marco enjoyed her company very much, the last thing on the young man's mind was marriage. He returned to Italy. The girl was despondent. It seemed as if the best thing to enter her life had been rudely snatched away from under her nose. Blind to the reality of her broken love affair, during May she followed in Marco's footsteps to Rome.

Carol stayed with the embarrassed boy's family for a while, but nevertheless made a favourable impression on Mrs Vitulano. Then fate intervened. Marco went off to do his national service. Now she knew the affair was really over.

Carol was a stranger in a strange land. But what was there back in Scotland? Unemployment, boredom? Her Italian was poor, but it was improving all the time. Then she heard that a wealthy family in Ortisei, near Bolzano, up in the Italian Alps, were looking for a nanny for their two-year-old son, Emanuele. Carol applied and was offered the position.

The Ricci family were ostentatious, and by British standards, the little boy was spoilt. When he was first introduced to Carol, he turned to his mother and said, 'My hand burns!' The boy never did grow to like her. But by now the wee lass was suffering more than a broken heart. She developed crippling abdominal pains which were diagnosed as appendicitis. Graciously, Emmanuella Ricci, the boy's mother, paid for Carol to have her appendix removed. But when she returned to the Ricci household, her problems were just beginning.

What began were the fires. Imagine a fire which can spring up at any time, anywhere. A fire which is *unnatural*. Were the fires which broke out in the wake of a young woman's heartbreak and physical distress unnatural? Or were they the product of a callous and disturbed mind?

Not only her young charge disliked Carol. A maid called Rosa developed an antagonism towards the girl. Many times she warned Mrs Ricci that she should never have employed the foreigner, and when strange things started to happen, Rosa was quick to blame Carol.

In a dark corridor of the villa hung an ancient painting of the Madonna. It had been there for years, undisturbed. Suddenly, with a loud crash, it fell to the floor. Rosa saw this as an omen connected in some way with the foreign girl. This was reinforced when a water boiler started to make gurgling noises, and, as Carol stood close by, an electricity meter went berserk. But it was the fires which seemed to confirm the accusations of the maid.

On 11 July 1982, the date of the first fire, Carol was alone in the house with the baby and the baby's grandfather. What exactly happened? No one seems to know. Carol was outside in the garden with Emanuele when the fire began. Nicole Annawabi, another of the Riccis' maids, was returning from the village when she noticed smoke pouring from a window of the house. Then she saw Carol clutching the child to her bosom, visibly distressed, shouting, 'Fire! Fire!' The old man was rescued, but £5000-worth of damage had been done to the villa.

In the meantime, the Morovers, friends of the Riccis, offered them shelter. But the fire followed them there too, and broke out not just once, but twice. The first occasion was a minor affair in a rubbish bin, but the second, on 16 July, was much more serious. In that, Mrs Ricci's brother narrowly escaped being trapped. A mattress which grandfather Ricci had been sleeping on had been found smouldering.

Both families were devastated. Carol was bemused and upset. But the finger of accusation had been pointed in her direction too often in the past. Carol was sacked from her position, even though there was no evidence to link her with any of the incidents. But within two weeks she had found a new job.

This time it was with a couple who worked with Italian television. They had a three-year-old daughter, Agnese, who was staying with her grandparents but becoming too much of a handful for them. The child and her grandparents were staying in a summer house on the island of Elba. With them Carol, it seemed, was destined to jump out of the frying pan and into the fire.

Even before Carol's arrival there was an 'atmosphere' in the house. Grandma Ancilla Cecchini was of the old generation. Corsican by birth, she believed a mother's place was at home with her child, looking after the house, doing the washing and preparing meals for her husband. This was despite the fact that her daughter-in-law's income had helped the Cecchinis climb the social ladder, and enabled them to afford the holiday home on Elba. Fundamentally the old lady did not agree with this 'modern' way of doing things, especially the hiring of nannies. She made this clear on many occasions. The last thing Ancilla Cecchini was prepared to tolerate was a child minder – especially a foreigner who hardly spoke the language.

Not long after Carol's arrival, 'things' began to happen. A small statue inexplicably fell from a shelf, a glass fruit bowl mysteriously fell to the floor, some circular markings were found on a wall. A three-tier cake stand fell from the dining room table with a terrible noise, but when Mrs Cecchini and a maid ran into the room, it was found to be standing upright and undamaged on the floor. The maid, Maria Annasuri, claimed to have seen a key turning in its lock by itself. The old Corsican grandmother had no doubts the villa had become haunted by a ghost. And she had no doubts who had brought the ghost into the house, even without knowing anything of the disastrous occurrences at the Riccis'. Carol, she informed everyone, was a witch! She possessed the Evil Eye.

Not long after came the first fire. The date was 1 August.

The child's parents were in Rome, working. Carol had done her best to keep out of the old woman's way, and as Mario Cecchini, the grandfather, was later to testify, the girl was relaxing in the sitting room after having dinner with them when the fire was discovered. It was Mario's mattress which was on fire.

But the worst was yet to come – just one day later. Little Agnese's mattress was found burning.

As Scottish advocate Lawrence Nisbet was to tell the media after Carol's arrest, 'She was having breakfast with other members of the family. The child was not burned because she was sleeping on the other side of the cot.'

Fortunately, the fire was discovered in time, but the house was in an uproar. Old grandmother Cecchini was now positive Carol was 'possessed by the Devil', and chased her around the villa, telling her she was a murderess. Carol escaped into the cellar, but not before the old woman had shaken her by the arms, shouting, 'It was you! It was you!'

But enough was enough. The parents returned, the police were called, and Carol Compton was arrested on the charge of 'attempted murder'. That was 2 August 1982. The real nightmare had just begun.

INVESTIGATION

'Carol Compton is a liar. She lied to her boyfriend and the families she worked for – especially the families. She showed them a face that was not a true face.' That was what public prosecutor Arturo Cindolo told the two judges and six members of the jury, during what *Glasgow Herald* newsman Andrew McCallum described as an 'onslaught'.

Was Carol Compton a liar who possessed a sweet and innocent façade which hid the evil heart of a pyromaniac, prepared to risk the lives of others and sacrifice the life of a three-year-old child? Could the fires have been started by someone else? Or was it just a string of crazy unbelievable coincidences? Was there another explanation entirely? *Were the fires supernatural?*

Carol was held awaiting trial in a dilapidated prison in Livorno, near Florence, and suffered further misery by mixing with drug addicts and women who tried to seduce her into lesbian activities. Yet there was no direct evidence to link her with any of her alleged crimes. She had no criminal record and was of good character. But this counted for nothing, because the Italian legal system is vastly different from that of the British, as McCallum explained in the *Glasgow Herald*.

There is no doubt Carol would have been quickly released in Scotland, but kidnappings, terrorism and other major crimes which threaten the Italian state are largely responsible for this outdated penal code. It survived the war Mussolini lost and the tumult which followed. Since then, political instability, bombings, killings and other outrages and scandals have made overhaul of the criminal law a painfully slow and reluctant business. It's particularly painful for the innocents locked away in prison; those who have not been charged or brought before any court and proven guilty.

Up to two years [in prison] have been spent by accused people subsequently released when a magistrate finally decided there was no case to answer. The whole cumbersome legal process is geared to ensuring that no big fish can slip through the net, but the relative minnows, some of whom should not have been in custody in the first place, suffer interminable delays as a spin-off.

Italy has no protective 110-day rule as has Scotland, where the law stipulates that an accused person in custody on petition proceedings must be brought to trial within that period. Although Carol Compton was no terrorist, the whole system is directed towards holding people so that they can be examined in detail, and there's never any hurry to release them from custody.

It was to be over sixteen months before Carol Compton was brought to trial. At the time of her arrest, Scottish advocate Lawrence Nisbet was on holiday in Italy. Nisbet lost no time in jumping in feet first. He offered his legal services to Carol, free of charge, if need be, then aligned himself with her Italian solicitor, Sergio Minervini.

Back home in Scotland, Nisbet was already painted quite a character. After graduating from Edinburgh University in 1970, he spent ten years at the bar before concentrating his interests on criminal rather than civil cases, taking part in a drugs trial – the biggest ever held in Scotland – at Edinburgh High Court.

Just before the Carol Compton affair, this dynamic advocate found himself at Edinburgh's Sheriff's Court – appearing for the defence, not the prosecution – where he was cleared of assaulting his wife. He was also in trouble with Sheriff Nigel Thomson for non-appearance at an earlier hearing, until it was explained he had been working in another court at the time. Nisbet typified the 'local boy does well' syndrome, having climbed the ladder of a bourgeois profession despite coming from a working-class background.

It is interesting that during the first two months of Carol's incarceration no one connected with her case was aware of the whole story. And who can blame her – guilty or innocent – for keeping mum? Her arrest was based solely on the allegations of the Cecchinis. The evidence against Carol was tenuous, so the girl was refused bail.

At the beginning of October 1982, magistrate Mr Luigi Di Franco was considering granting Carol provisional bail. A priest, Father Nolan from Florence, even arranged for a hostel run by nuns to accommodate her. But these plans were for nothing. The application was turned down, because, according to Di Franco, psychiatric and forensic tests had not been completed.

Then the real bombshell hit. The Riccis came forward. On top of the attempted murder charge already being considered, two more charges were now receiving the attention of the magistrate. In the end the charges were refined to one of attempted murder of little Agnese, and five charges of arson.

Now there was absolutely no chance of an early release. Carol Compton was in the hands of the Italian legal system and the media circus, already descending on Livorno in search of cheap thrills. Millions of people across Europe and the rest of the world were told that Carol was 'suspected of pyrokinesis, the ability to start fires by psychic means'.

The British media painted an extreme picture of a legal system out of *Alice in Wonderland*, and a society still entrenched in the superstitions of the middle ages, prepared to put a young girl on trial for 'witchcraft'. Yet this patently was not the case. Whatever the merit of the evidence, Carol was on trial for arson and attempted murder. There had been rumblings about the incidents being paranormal, but where had the silly 'witchcraft' tag come from?

Serena Macbeth, a television film maker, was on holiday in Italy at the time Carol was arrested and became closely involved with the case by offering her services as an interpreter free to Sergio Minervini.

'Minervini told me it had all started as a joke. While discussing the case with Nisbet he had remarked, "Scotland's full of witches, isn't it?" Then at a press conference, Nisbet told reporters that Carol was "on trial for witchcraft". It spread like wildfire, and soon all the papers were filled with this nonsense about "the witchcraft trial". Minervini was very embarrassed.'

We asked Ian Cameron of the *Daily Record* about this. 'Yes, there was a press conference and I think it was there that reference to the girl being tried for practising "witchcraft" was mentioned. Of course such a statement was guaranteed to make headlines, and I think it's fair to say that this contributed to Carol's lengthy stay in custody.'

But what did Minervini think about his Scottish colleague? We invited Serena Macbeth to comment. 'I think Minervini thought Nisbet might have been better employed concerning himself more with his client and less with the media.'

Sometime later, the Scottish end of the defence was moved to another solicitor, a Mr Nicol Hosie of Aberdeen.

But surely Italian newspapers and television played more than a passive role in drumming up the 'witchcraft' angle? Serena smiled. Half Italian herself, she knows that country intimately. 'Contrary to the impression given by the British tabloids, the Italians are *not* a bunch of superstitious peasants. In my experience, generally the opposite is true. The British are much worse!'

One has to admit this comment is not without foundation.

Britain had a Witchcraft Act which was not repealed until 1951, when it was replaced by the Fraudulent Mediums Act. The case which brought this change about caused quite as big an uproar as the one being played out in 'superstitious' Italy. This concerned another Scot – medium Helen Duncan.

Helen, born in 1898, earned quite a reputation for herself as a medium in the 1930s and 1940s. She convinced thousands of people that the dead could return in a quasi-physical form generated by 'ectoplasm'. This is a substance said to emanate from a medium's body.

Trouble began in May 1933, when she was fined £10 after claims that her spirit guide, 'Peggy', was nothing more than a woman's undervest! Then in 1944, after a police raid, she and three others were arrested. Eventually, after some confusion, the Witchcraft Act of 1735 was cited, and newspapers heralded it as 'the trial of the century'.

Conducted at the Old Bailey, the trial lasted seven days, and ended with a guilty verdict of conspiracy to contravene the Witchcraft Act. The medium received nine months' imprisonment, after the judge remarked he had not been concerned whether or not 'genuine manifestations of the kind are possible ... this court has nothing whatever to do with such abstract questions.'

Helen Duncan was the last person to be tried under the Witchcraft Act. After her release she continued her seances until 1956. Then, during another police raid, she was rudely disturbed while in a trance-like state and was taken ill. According to spiritualists, it is dangerous to disturb a medium under trance. Just over five weeks later, Helen Duncan was dead.

But Carol Compton's position was not the same as that of compatriot Helen Duncan thirty-eight years before. Carol was not claiming mediumistic powers, or anything much at all – except that she was not guilty of all charges. She gave the impression of an innocent caught up in a Kafkaesque nightmare quite beyond her control.

However, is it any wonder that such terms as 'witchcraft', 'supernatural' and 'paranormal' were being bandied about? It really was too coincidental that fires of this unknown nature should break out in three different houses in as many weeks. As Arturo Cindolo, the public prosecutor, quite rightly commented, without actually endorsing a paranormal component: 'She is the common factor in all these fires. The families are different and the places were far apart from each other. But Miss Compton was there and so were the fires. It is too much to speak of "coincidence".'

The trial finally began on 12 December 1983. Immediately it caused a sensation which rippled around the world. Because of the pre-trial publicity, the courtroom was packed with over seventy TV, radio, magazine and newspaper journalists. They were not to be disappointed.

Carol was escorted into the court by armed soldiers, then locked into a steel cage. Ian Cameron remembers it vividly. 'I was horrified. It caused an incredible reaction amongst my colleagues. Pamela Compton – the girl's mother, who had flown over especially for the trial – rushed over to her daughter with pressmen hot on her heels, elbowing one another out of the way, climbing on tables, over chairs. I was pushed aside by one man, cameras were flashing everywhere.'

During this mêlée, Carol was reported as shouting defiantly through the bars at journalists: 'I'm ready for the fight to prove my innocence.' But the chaos continued even when the officials entered.

According to Andrew McCallum, 'Flashbulbs greeted court president Guido Galligani, the second judge, eight court assessors, the public prosecutor and a host of other officials.'

They immediately turned and left with the fourteen prosecution and defence witnesses, the president shouting loudly about photographers. For the next two hours the courtroom never did settle down, and occasionally uproar erupted again. During a second stormy adjournment, president Galligani shouted at police, 'Why should I have to deal with photographers? It's your job!'

'The police went around confiscating camera film,' Ian Cameron told us, adding with a grin, 'but all they got were rolls of unused film.'

After an impassioned plea by her defence lawyer, Galligani agreed to release Carol from the cage and a seat was found for her next to her legal advisers. But why was she caged in the first place? This was not, as some British media sources speculated, because the 'superstitious' Italian judges were afraid of her. In fact the cage had been constructed a few years before for the trial of Red Brigade terrorists, and had been there ever since.

Andrew McCallum said, 'None of this would have happened in a British court of justice. During the whole course of the trial people were coming and going as they pleased, smoking, interrupting. It was quite an education.'

At one point the prosecutor rowed with a judge and slammed his books down in temper, poor acoustics made the hearing of vital evidence difficult, the interpreter burst into tears shouting that everyone was picking on her, and Mrs Ricci complained loudly about the inconvenience of waiting to give evidence, and the expense of travelling from Rome.

During the second day, Carol and one of the Riccis' maids, Nicole Annawabi, started fighting before the bench. Nicole was making a statement when Carol snatched the microphone from her, and told everyone she was lying, before Nicole grabbed it back. After that incident, the president decided he had had enough for one day, no doubt regretting his decision to allow Carol out of the terrorists' cage.

The interpretation of certain words caused much fuss too. In particular an argument lasted for half an hour over what exactly was meant by the term 'tea'. Apparently, Carol was making 'tea' when one of the fires started in another part of the building. The official interpreter advised the court that Carol had been making a *pot* of tea.

Serena Macbeth explained, 'As it takes about five minutes to make a pot of tea, this would mean, in theory, Carol would have had plenty of time to start the fire. In fact Carol had been making *tea* – a late afternoon meal – half an hour of a job, diminishing the possibility that that particular fire could have been down to her.'

But events reached the height of farce on the third day, when attention turned to an old woman dressed in black muttering from the public gallery. Then to everyone's astonishment the woman shuffled towards Carol, muttering incantations and holding high a large wooden crucifix, like a refugee from a Count Dracula film.

Waiting journalists eagerly pounced on her after her ejection by the police. Her name was Ciara Lobina, and despite the theatrics, she was a well-known clairvoyant and faith healer. The devil, she said, had come to her in a dream, with knowledge that both Carol and her mother, Pamela, were possessed by the spirit of a young eighteenth-century witch who had 'given them the power of fire'.

Diana Hutchinson of the *Daily Mail* described how the old woman had managed to yank back Carol's head and throw holy water over Pamela Compton before she was restrained. The press dubbed Ciara Lobina 'The Black Nun' and went away with another smash headline to titillate their readers.

In an attempt by the defence to steer the burden of blame away from Carol, they called 22-year-old Theresa Hunter to give evidence.

Theresa left the Cecchinis' employ three days before Carol took over. She spoke of the grandmother, Ancilla Cecchini, leaving smouldering cigarette ends around the house, as well as faulty and overloaded power sockets. Theresa was in no doubt who *really* was to blame. In a statement which was never followed up, the ex-nanny claimed that three other nannies had also left because of inexplicable fires. 'If I had stayed, I would probably have been accused of the crimes Carol is charged with today,' she told the court.

Later, Ian Cameron interviewed her. 'The grandmother was really weird. She hated nannies. In fact she may have started the fires. She used to smoke a lot and sometimes left lighted cigarettes around, forgetting where she'd put them.'

But this attempt could not possibly succeed for two reasons. Firstly there was no evidence to link Ancilla Cecchini with the fires, and secondly it meant ignoring the incidents at the other two locations.

The trial lasted five days. The jury, six people especially selected from all over Italy, were out for six and a half hours. At the end of this, the president announced a verdict of not proven of the attempted murder charge, but guilty of two charges of arson and one of attempted fire-raising.

Carol was given a two-and-a-half-year jail sentence, but the president immediately ordered her release because of the seventeen months already spent in prison awaiting trial. Not surprisingly, by the following day, Carol and her mother were back home in Scotland.

This conclusion was viewed as expedient and inevitable. The affair had caused much embarrassment to the Italians. Yet the guilty verdict, based on the evidence, or lack of it, did seem a nonsense. Bob Rickard, editor of the paranormal journal *Fortean Times*, summed it up thus: 'In pressing for a sentence of seven years, the prosecutor reiterated that, "This trial is not about witchcraft. We are here to talk about facts, not fantasies." And yet very little could be established, for no witnesses saw Carol set the fires, nor was she in their immediate vicinity when they started.'

This view was supported by journalist Robin Lustig in an article published in the *Observer* magazine of 16 January 1983, entitled 'Witch-Hunt In Italy'. This included testimonies confirming that few if any of the fires broke out in the presence of Carol, and further credence was added to the other, poltergeist-like, activity.

Glasgow Herald man Andrew McCallum, while remaining cautious, admitted that no one in that courtroom had supplied the answers. The verdict was based on nothing more than speculation. However, reporter Ian Cameron was inclined to agree with the jury's conclusion. 'You've got to remember that at the time the girl was very disturbed. She was in a strange country, hardly spoke the language and was recovering from a broken love affair. There was a lot of pressure. The fires could just have been a cry for attention. I don't think anything supernatural happened at all.'

In Italy, there are no sub judice rules, and this was why *20/20 Vision*, the company Serena Macbeth worked for, were able to film Carol in Livorno prison, and her mother, for a documentary destined for Channel 4. In 'The Trial of Carol Compton', Carol resisted the paranormal theory, and her mother had this to say: 'Utter rubbish! My Carol is being used as a scapegoat for other people's mistakes. My Carol is a normal, happy, carefree girl.'

During her incarceration, one of the investigating judges ordered Carol to be examined by two psychiatrists. They concluded that 'Carol's mental state was not in question'. The irony is that if she had been judged as mentally unstable, no charges could have been made against her.

With even Carol Compton, at least publicly, unsupportive of the paranormal option, just how much of a viable proposition was it? If it was a real alternative, was there any proof?

Amazing though it seems, there *was* scientific proof indicative of this, presented in the courtroom. This took the form of forensic tests results which should have been the cornerstone of any verdict reached by the jury.

The first expert to give evidence was a fire officer from

Bolzano, who had examined the sites of the three fires involving the Ricci family. He noted the peculiarity of the fires, which burned downwards. Some months earlier he had told Serena Macbeth and her British film crew that the ferocity of the big fire in Ortisei was indicative of a fire which had been burning for hours – not minutes. This man proudly boasted of his thirty-eight years' experience of fire investigation.

In court, Professor Vitolo Nicolo of Pisa University added a wealth of empirical information. 'In all my forty-five years' experience of this kind of investigation I have never seen fires like this before. They were created by an intense source of heat, *but not by a naked flame*.'

He also agreed with what the fire officer from Bolzano had said, in that the Cecchini fires too had burned only the surface of the material. 'Strangely, both mattresses had been burned only on the surface and at the same spot. The burn marks could have been caused by a hot iron but not by a cigarette lighter, a match or any naked flame. Both fires had the same characteristics; great heat but no flames. I have never seen anything like it before.'

Although the two mattresses examined by Professor Nicolo were made of different materials – wool and horsehair – they both burned in the same peculiar way.

'They were only burned on the outside, not the inside,' he added. The professor agreed with defence lawyer Sergio Minervini that he had found no evidence to link Carol with the fires. This crucial scientific evidence should have stood up strongly against the wild speculations of various witnesses, but it was all but ignored by the court.

While making their documentary, the *20/20 Vision* crew hired forensic expert Dr Keith Borer to carry out their own independent tests on identical – albeit scaled down – wool and horsehair mattresses. In particular he was interested in the fourth fire – the first to occur at the Cecchinis' holiday villa – where the grandfather's bed caught fire. It had scorched in a long even strip along the entire length of one side. It had already been verified that no inflammable liquids had been used, so Dr Borer struck a match and applied it to the bottom edge of the trial mattress.

It took many minutes to light – minutes which Carol had not possessed – then very slowly burned in an irregular upwards pattern, creating insufficient smoke to alert anyone outside the bedroom. Borer freely admitted he was stumped. He was further mystified by the first fire at Ortisei which had caused an estimated £5000 of damage. The wooden stool, where apparently the fire had started, was only slightly damaged while the rest of the room was destroyed. And seemingly the fire had 'jumped' a couple of feet lower and sideways into the drawer of a cupboard. Dr Borer had no answers, not even an ounce of an idea to form the most speculative of scenarios. Yet when he was asked about the paranormal option, he had this to say. 'The facts don't quite fit, so we resurrect the paranormal label. Maybe there are some facts missing. Perhaps if we had all the facts we wouldn't need the paranormal label?'

As someone else said, the absence of facts is nothing more than unexplained facts to most scientists. But as we discovered in some of the other cases we researched for this book, establishment judges and coroners are prepared to ignore hard scientific evidence when it points in a direction they are trained to ignore. They want mundane 'logical' answers, and when they are lacking, other, hearsay evidence is made to 'fit'. That way, no one rocks the boat, and everyone sleeps at night.

Having ascertained Carol Compton was not a pyromaniac, not one of her accusers could come up with a valid motive for why she should go around starting fires in the first place. Weakly it was suggested she started them in order to get the sack, and thus be sent back to Rome in order to be with her boyfriend, but this was a nonsense. Apart from the obvious fact that Carol could simply have handed in her notice, Marco explained that they had been apart many times, even in Scotland, and besides, she knew he was away doing his national service.

Carol, it seemed, was not quite as heartbroken as the media had painted. Marco's mother had in fact attended the trial, and after the girl's release said to reporters, 'I've never believed Carol could commit such terrible feats like trying to kill a defenceless child. I'm glad she's free, and I hope she can begin anew again and find happiness.'

Perhaps if Minervini had stuck his neck out and explored the paranormal alternative, his client would have been acquitted of all charges. Instead he left her open to a maximum twenty-one-year prison sentence. Was this why it was reported that Lawrence Nisbet had 'been at odds with Mr Minervini over how the case should be handled'? Although it was given little publicity, Minervini had at his disposal a body of evidence gathered from experts around the world citing similar case histories to that of the Compton affair. The defence lawyer decided to ignore it. Was it worth the gamble? Without playing the paranormal ace, those searching for a conventional fire-raiser and willing to ignore the forensic experts were bound to find Carol Compton guilty. As already pointed out, she was the only common denominator. There had to be a connection.

When the story first broke in Britain on a television news bulletin, paranormal researcher Dr Hugh Pincott quickly contacted ITN and obtained details of the Scottish lawyer handling the case – Lawrence Nisbet. Pincott immediately offered his help. Dr Pincott is a founder of ASSAP – the Association for the Scientific Study of Anomalous Phenomena, and a respected local politician.

We had no access to first-hand evidence and could only assess events as reported, somewhat sensationally, by the press. Nevertheless, there seemed to be elements in common with the large number of similar events that have been reported over the years.

The scientific literature on cases like Carol's stretches back into the past century and fills libraries. Furthermore, there are specialists – medical consultants, psychologists and professors at universities throughout the world – who have spent life-times studying the subject.

We wanted to ensure that the defence lawyers had access to the very best possible information should they wish to use it as a line of defence. That they did not pursue it was entirely their prerogative. ASSAP did not want to promote any particular line, but the brief was available, and that is what was important.

When we asked Dr Pincott for more details, this is what he had to say:

Then responsibility for the Scottish side moved to another lawyer – a Mr Nicol Hosie. I wrote him a similar letter to the one sent to Nisbet, offering to help with any specialist parapsychological information. But Sr Minervini preferred that the 'poltergeist' angle be played right down, in contradistinction to the press, who blew it right up. Nisbet had in conversation referred to a local forensic report which appeared to indicate there was no external source for the fires. I offered to obtain confidential professional comment on the report for the defence.

Mr Hosie appreciated the offer of assistance and said he would confer with Sr Minervini. He thought Sr Minervini might consider our involvement as and when charges were brought. He also mentioned he had been asked to refuse disclosure of the contents of the forensic report at this stage.

By coincidence, Hugh Pincott discovered that Italian psychologist Dr Paola Giovetti, who was helping Minervini and had access to Carol, was also a good friend of colleague Guy Playfair, so the two men teamed up to form the UK side of what Pincott describes as 'this interesting international network'.

At an early stage I was approached by a Scottish journalist, Ms Eilean Ross, who knew the Compton family. Alas Eilean died a few months later, but her contribution to Carol's welfare was enormous. She was writing regular pieces for the press, but she was in full possession of all the confidential information which never once was even hinted at publicly. It was she who was the go-between with the unco-operative Compton family, and she provided the introduction to the MEP, Mr Alasdair Hutton.

Hutton felt quite strongly about the whole affair, and even if the defence lawyers did not wish to be associated with the parapsychological approach, he was quite prepared to acquaint the Italian authorities 'at ministerial level' with the opinions of 'academic and professional people, properly qualified in medicine, psychology and other scientific disciplines, who are well acquainted with the serious literature on poltergeist activity, particularly the aspects related to psychokinesis.'

Dr Pincott and Guy Playfair approached a whole range of parapsychologists, and the result was a forty-page dossier sent to Hutton. Its effect, if any, on the Italian authorities, is not known. However, submissions were obtained from the following academics:

Dr Jean Dierkens, University of Mons, Belgium
Professor John Hasted, Birkbeck College, London
Professor Archie Roy, Glasgow University
Dr John Beloff, University of Edinburgh
Dr Derek Lawden, University of Aston
Mr Arthur North, Polytechnic of North London
Professor Arthur Ellison, City University
Professor Hans Bender, University of Freiburg
Professor George Owen, University of Toronto
Dr James McHury, University of Dundee
Dr Hernani Guimaraes, Brazilian Institute of Psychiatry
Dr Alfred Kranz, a French neuropsychiatrist

But what exactly are 'poltergeist phenomena'?

The poltergeist phenomenon can encompass different manifestations of varying intensity. These manifestations consist basically of the following: auditory effects such as rappings and knockings; movement of objects observed or unobserved; destruction of objects; disappearance and reappearance of objects; the slaughter of family pets; mysterious fires; disembodied voices; footsteps; apparitions; strange smells. Each alleged case exhibits one or more of these characteristics, but very rarely most of them.

Poltergeist cases have been well documented by people beyond reproach. The Church has no doubts concerning the 'reality' of this type of phenomenon. Each diocese has its own exorcist in England. When the authors interviewed biologist Dr Lyall Watson, he spoke of the hundred or so cases he had investigated – sometimes witnessing the phenomena himself – from all around the world.

But what of those cases comparable to Carol Compton's? Even as Carol was languishing in jail, on the Indian Ocean island of Réunion another set of mysterious fires was breaking out. The girl at the centre in this instance was twelve years old, and her name was Nadine Calojine.

The first outbreak was on 16 February 1983, when a neighbour's flat was devastated by an unexplained fire while the owners were out. Just two days later another fire gutted the flat completely. Not long after, the fire brigade answered a call at Nadine's flat. There they discovered a mattress on fire. Then over the following week, including Monday, the young girl's clothes caught fire repeatedly, two mattresses burned, and some linen in a cupboard was discovered alight. There was speculation 'of children playing with matches', but nothing was resolved.

According to documentation, the phenomenon is not new and has been around for years.

In Thurston's *Ghosts and Poltergeists*, published in 1953, the author cites the case of the Daggy household from 1889. Woodcock, the investigator, made a statement based on the testimony of seventeen witnesses to the effect that 'fires have broken out spontaneously throughout the house, as many as eight occurring in one day, six being in the house and two outside; that the window curtains were burned, this happening in broad daylight whilst the family and neighbours were in the house.'

The *New York Herald* of 6 January 1895 told of the 'many fires' which had plagued the house of Adam Colwell of Brooklyn during 4 and 5 January. The final outbreak razed the house to the ground.

Police officers witnessed furniture bursting into flames; firemen reported that the fires were of unknown origin. As in many other cases of this nature, a young woman became the prime suspect. The Fire Marshal, in referring to Colwell's stepdaughter Rhoda, aged sixteen, said: 'It might be thought the child Rhoda started two of the fires, but she cannot be considered guilty of the others, as she was being questioned when some of them began. I do not want to be quoted as a believer in the supernatural, but I have no explanation to offer, as to the cause of the fires, nor of the throwing around of furniture.'

Colwell stated that he, his wife and stepdaughter had been all together when they heard a crash. A large empty parlour stove was discovered fallen to the floor. While Colwell was out, four pictures fell from the walls, and on his return he smelled smoke. A bed was found to be on fire.

A police officer helped put out the fire, then, while still in the house, he saw some wallpaper start to burn. A detective, Sergeant Dunn, arrived. He witnessed another fire and saw a heavy lamp fall from its hook.

Finally the house burned down, and the family were taken to the police station. There, a Captain Rhoads of the Greenpoint Precinct made this curious statement. 'The people we arrested had nothing to do with the strange fires. The more I look into it, the deeper the mystery. So far I can attribute it to no other cause than a supernatural agency. Why, the fires broke out under the very noses of the men I sent to investigate.'

Sergeant Dunn added, 'There were things that happened before my eyes that I did not believe were possible.'

Yet only the following day came an amazing turnaround.

The *New York Herald* sported this headline: 'Policemen And Firemen Artfully Tricked By a Pretty Young Girl.' Readers will experience an acute sense of déjà vu on hearing the following. A Mr Hope had come forward and claimed that while Rhoda had been in his employ as a housemaid, between November and December, four mysterious fires had occurred.

Now it was obvious, surely? The coincidence was too great to ignore. Rhoda *had* started the fires after all! However, the girl must have employed conjuring tricks which even today would put magician Paul Daniels to shame, skilfully causing pictures to fall and large objects to move without being anywhere near. Fires were made to break out right under the noses of experienced police and fire officers.

To account for this 'trickery', Captain Rhoads devised an astonishing theory. Everyone agreed that Rhoda was very pretty, and everyone knows what effect pretty girls have on healthy specimens of manhood. In this instance Rhoda had turned her family, police officers and firemen blind, had reduced their intellect to that of chimpanzees, and raised their gullibility factor to the stage where they would accept such whimsical notions as 'supernatural agencies'. Obviously, while Sergeant Dunn and his fire-fighting colleagues were quaking at the knees and foaming at the mouth, Rhoda was busy tossing matches everywhere and knocking over furniture.

Nevertheless, even Rhoda must have realized that in some way she was connected with the incidents. The girl became very frightened, and the police 'advised' her to tell the truth. Rhoda did as she was advised and claimed she had caused the poltergeist-like phenomena in order to force the family to move to another neighbourhood. How this ties in with the previous fires at Mr Hope's house was never explained.

Perhaps the truth is simply that American girls are not made of the same tough stuff as those brought up in Scotland.

But why is there in the majority of these cases almost always a young man or woman being blamed for these occurrences?

As early as 1930, parapsychologist Hereward Carrington wrote: 'An energy seems to be radiated from the body . . . when the sexual energies are blossoming into maturity . . . it would almost seem as if these energies instead of taking the normal course . . . find this curious means of externalization.'

A credible scientific hypothesis, on the fringes of scientific understanding, and thus beyond the rigid boundaries of establishment acceptance, is that of psychokinesis – the alleged ability of some people to cause inanimate objects to move with some unknown energy directed from the mind. Poltergeist manifestations, according to this reasoning, are nothing more than spontaneous involuntary psychokinesis – an anarchic, unconscious and uncontrolled demonstration of inner hysteria.

Scientists Professor Hans Eysenck and Dr Carl Sargent, while commenting on poltergeist phenomena, made these final observations: 'So what can we learn from the poltergeist? It would be surprising if we got a neat, reliable, coherent story. The one thing we *do* learn is that there are a core of cases in which the evidence for psychokinesis is very strong.'

Did the fires at three Italian villas have a supernatural cause? Or was Carol Compton just exceptionally cunning? Ian Cameron thought it fair to deduce that Carol's emotional state could have acted as a catalyst for her to light fires to gain attention. But, ironically, according to the parapsychologists, internal emotional distress is also necessary to trigger off poltergeist manifestations.

But after all the options have been considered, two very clear facts still stand out. Carol Compton is the *only* common denominator. And no matter how hard the public prosecutors tried, not one shred of evidence was uncovered to link Carol directly with any of the incidents. In the normal way of things.

3

The Spectre of Death

Ken Edwards yawned. It had been a long day. The job was all right – he quite enjoyed it – but being a service engineer entailed a lot of travelling about, concentration in heavy traffic, changing gear up and down like he was a one-armed bandit junkie. From early in the morning he had been at it, then had a quick evening meal, a wash and change, before going off to his regular union meeting at Sale, just south of Manchester.

Now it was late, and dark, but he was on his way home. That made him feel good. The M62 shone black in the van headlights, snaking through the wastes of Chat Moss – ten miles of desolate peat bog lying between the big city and Warrington. Ken knew the route like the back of his hand. He knew exactly how long it was, and what time he would reach home.

One and a half miles from the end of his journey, he indicated, and left the motorway at Risley, using an unsign-posted slip road, a short cut used mainly by the locals. He had left the meeting, after a drink or two, at about 11 P.M. He glanced at his watch. It was approaching 11.30.

The van rattled along the deserted road, the planned new housing estate not yet built. There were no other vehicles, just himself, his thoughts of his wife Barbara, and the warm bed awaiting him.

To his left stretched a bleak landscape – thousands of acres of former Ministry of Defence property, a generation before brimming with life; a life which danced with the machinery of death. Ken knew that beyond the glare of his headlights huddled long-abandoned World War Two ordnance factories. Now at last they were to be demolished, making way for new development.

The tall, likeable man behind the wheel changed down, negotiated a small island close to the AA Relay Station, then slowly continued along what was now Daten Avenue. Up ahead was an embankment skirted with trees and bushes, on his right. Beyond that was a university research unit into sensory deprivation. To his left, about level with the embankment on the opposite side, was a ten-foot-high chain-linked security fence. This surrounded land belonging to the Atomic Energy Authority.

Suddenly, about a hundred yards ahead, on top of the embankment, his headlights picked out an impossible-looking figure. His eyes were immediately glued to it.

Automatically he slowed the van until it was at a standstill at the side of the road. His mind was uncomprehending, suddenly snatched out of its reverie of bed, and his weekend off. He tried to place the figure within the cosy framework of his day to day life. Could it be someone – anyone – even at that late hour, climbing in such a peculiar fashion down the embankment?

The man in the car was like a rabbit hypnotized by a snake. Helpless. He realized that if it was not a prankster, he was trapped out there on the lonely road. Ken sat entranced, as the bizarre event unfolded before him.

As it climbed down the steep incline, the thing had its arms stretched out before it, like someone in a farce sleepwalking. Ken realized this stance was impossible, which added to his fear. One would have to balance *backwards* in order not to topple over. At the bottom the figure moved across the wide grass verge to the edge of the road, then stopped. Ken had a much better view of it now, and he felt panic rising in the pit of his stomach as he realized that whatever the thing was, *it was not a fellow human being*.

The creature was tall – about seven feet – with a broad

body. And, like something from a nightmare, its arms grew out of the top of its shoulders. The whole of the body, except for the head, was covered in a silver-coloured boilersuit-type garment. The head was encased in a black balaclava-style helmet, as round as a football, two circular eyes the only visible features.

Ken Edwards sat crouched in his seat, hands tightly gripping the wheel, wishing fervently he could disappear.

After pausing for a short while the entity began crossing the wide road. It seemed rather ill-equipped for this simple manoeuvre. The entire body moved very stiffly, walking from the hips; there was no evidence of knee joints at all. Ken was shocked as it stopped in the middle of the road, just yards away from him. Slowly, as if aware of him for the first time, its head began to swivel to face the van.

Now the eyes fastened on him. The man was terrified, unable to run or drive away, sweating, clutching at the wheel. All he could do was stay put and take whatever was in store. From the eyes projected two pencil-slim shafts of light, which pierced the windscreen and fastened on him. This seemed to last about a minute, the bright lights pinning him like a butterfly in a glass case, causing havoc in the vehicle's electrical system. It was only later it was discovered that the van's radio-transceiver set had suffered irreparable damage.

Suddenly it was over. The head slowly turnwd to face forward again, and the thing moved with its stiff gait across the road on to the far verge. The fence blocked its progress. What would it do now? Turning left would bring it even closer to the van. Turn right, Ken prayed, turn right! It did neither. Instead it lifted up its arms once more, lowered them, *then walked right through the metal fence*.

At that moment of contact the fence ceased to be an impenetrable barrier. Matter passed through matter, and the spectral entity shambled silently up the incline beyond to be swallowed by the darkness.

Ken Edwards did not know what to do, his mind was in chaos, his entire life shaken to pieces in the space of a few minutes. He had met an unknown, unfathomable thing. He had fallen victim to something which society claimed did not exist. Was he going insane? Surely not, it was much too real . . .

Somehow he managed to get the van into gear, but only retained a vague memory of the drive home. Even more bewildering, the experience had seemed to last just a few minutes, but it was almost 12.30 A.M. by the time he parked the van in the drive – a discrepancy of roughly forty-five minutes.

He entered the bungalow and, uncharacteristically, went straight for the drinks cabinet. Barbara, his wife, followed him, already worried because he was late, and now convinced something dreadful had occurred, perhaps a serious road accident.

'What's wrong, Ken, what on earth's happened?'

He spilled a generous measure of whisky into a chunky glass and took a gulp, nearly choking as it hit the back of his throat. She quickly noted his blood-drained hands and staring eyes which focused on her as if he were struggling to reply.

'I've seen a silver man,' he blurted, then, when he had calmed a little, told her the whole story.

Barbara could not believe it. How could she? It was insane. Yet her husband was normally so level headed, and he certainly was not a liar. Something terrifying had occurred, that much was obvious.

Sleep was a hundred miles from his thoughts, but he began undressing for bed, his mind striving for the return of normalcy. He stopped. This was useless. He had to face up to it, take the ridicule, tell people what had happened. He had to be believed.

Barbara looked up, startled, as he began dressing again.

'I think I'd better go to the police,' he mumbled. 'Will you take me?'

He huddled into the passenger seat as she drove him to Padgate police station. The officers on duty thought at first it was a prank; 17 March was St Patrick's Day. Then they too noticed the pallor of his skin, the nervous tremor in his voice, and the impassioned concern of his wife. Crazy though the story was, Ken Edwards won them over, and they decided to mount an investigation.

While the couple waited, a call was put through to the Atomic Energy Authority who owned the land beyond the ten-foot chain-linked fence. Barbara returned home, and Ken reluctantly agreed to go with the officers back to the eerie silence of Daten Avenue. There, a surprise awaited him. The police car was met by a gathering of about twenty-five uniformed men – security officers from the plant.

They clustered round as he repeated his story, pointing out where the spectral entity had come down the embankment on one side of the road, before disappearing up the other, after first walking through a solid metal fence.

There was no smirking nor derision. They were all armed with batons, and several of the men fingered them nervously. The fence was examined and found to be undamaged, and a general search of the area was made. Nothing was found. Ken pointed out that the figure had last been seen heading in the general direction of some trees.

So convinced were they that he was telling the truth, that all of them refused to go into the trees and search.

This was far from the end of the matter. Within hours, the police were to release the story to the press, creating an invasion of reporters and weird religious cultists who would stamp all over Ken's privacy. There were the strange phone calls from people who did not exist, a second appearance by the thing in Daten Avenue, and finally, one last, sad event.

INVESTIGATION

In the *Bolton Evening News* of 6 June 1987 local UFO researcher Steve Balon was quoted on the Ken Edwards case. His comments appear to have been based upon second-hand information. The journalist referred to mysterious sightings in what he called the 'famed Bolton triangle' (of which, despite our extensive background in this field and the fact that we both live nearby, neither of us have ever heard).

As for the figure Ken Edwards saw, this was accounted for as 'contact with an alien being' because, the story claimed, 'No power on earth can produce [such things] . . . They have to come from beyond this planet.'

Perhaps Steve Balon will be proven right one day. But it seems to us an extremely premature conclusion to jump to on the strength of what we know about the events at Risley. It should be added that the following investigation is based not on second-hand material but solely upon work that we, the authors, did at the time of the events and in the years since. Peter Hough visited Ken and Barbara Edwards within a few days of the incident and Jenny Randles spent some time with them a couple of weeks later, when the furore had died down. She also maintained periodic contact with Ken, talking to him every six months or so during the years after the encounter. As it happened this proved significant.

For the purpose of this chapter a good deal of reinvestigation occurred, in an effort to discover if there finally was a solution to this bizarre case which, as you will see, had very tragic consequences.

To be fair to Mr Balon, he was only repeating what many people had assumed in 1978. The story had found its way very quickly to the local press, the *Warrington Guardian*, when a routine call to the Padgate police for any local-interest story produced the unlikely tale of the events on Daten Avenue just hours after they occurred. On that Saturday morning both the police and Ken Edwards had misread the situation, unaware of the interest likely to be provoked by the matter. Ken had not given the police permission to release his name, but when the media began to call he was prepared to talk.

The local newspaper had quickly seen the potential of what was being alleged. The country was then agog with UFO fever; a film entitled *Close Encounters of the Third Kind* had received a royal première less than a week earlier, on 13 March. In this highly successful Steven Spielberg fantasy the UFOs wreak havoc in an Indiana town. The fairy lights and spectacular spaceships depicted are rooted in a sort of reality. UFO expert Dr J. Allen Hynek was the consultant (and in many ways the catalyst) for the entire movie. The odd title actually comes from his classification scheme: an encounter of the third kind being when someone meets an alien entity!

Naturally, in many folks' eyes, this was exactly what had happened to Ken Edwards. The press had described the Spielberg movie plot. The *Daily Express* had even run a 'UFO Bureau' during February and were swamped by hundreds of calls and letters reporting sightings. And the *Warrington Guardian* were not steering clear of the subject either. They had their own series to discuss local UFO events.

On the day of the Risley sighting they published an article with the daft title 'Secret File on UFO Invasion'. Labelled an 'Exclusive', it revealed for the first time the secret files of the mysterious UFO group TRACE, from Winsford. TRACE stands for 'Technical Registration of Ariel Contacts Encountered' – for some reason amateur UFO hunters love silly acronyms like that. However, despite considerable efforts, we have not been able to find any evidence that TRACE were ever heard from again over the next decade.

According to the article, Roy Everall of the British Astronomical Association ran the group. It had been set up in 1972 after a spate of UFO sightings in the town. Indeed it was these same sightings which precipitated Jenny Randles' decision to become a UFO investigator. However, of the sightings that she investigated almost all were explained as aircraft going into Manchester Airport.

Despite this awkward fact, Mr Everall told the *Guardian* about his explosive hidden dossier built up since that flap. It had convinced him that Winsford was 'the UFO hot-bed of the country', a declaration that time has sadly failed to vindicate.

But the most important item in this half-page spread was a log of local sightings garnered by the Aetherius Society, whose Warrington branch leader, Mrs Phyllis Henderson, was quoted as saying that the UFOs were piloted by advanced technologists from other planets in the solar system.

The Aetherians are a strange bunch. Officially registered as a religion in the USA, their role in the Risley saga is intriguing. They were formed in the mid-fifties by George King, a London cabbie, who received word that he was to rescue the universe from a marauding meteorite then on its way to chomp through Earth. By taking command of the defeated fleet of Martian and Venusian spaceships he won the day, received the highest award available and became nominated for the interplanetary parliament as representative for some backwater planet called Earth. He then began to receive telepathic messages from the aliens which he spoke into a tape recorder. These vocalizations (which naturally sound not dissimilar to George King) supposedly came from places like Mars Sector Six, although some were from Jesus, in his new home on Venus. They believe in all this sincerely.

This might all sound quaintly amusing thirty years later, when we know full well that nobody lives on Mars or Venus and such 'Dan Dare' adventures are improbable. However, it cannot be over-emphasized that this group still command extraordinary respect. As we write (in late 1987) the BBC are planning a serious documentary about them, and they are often billed as representative of UFO researchers. They are no such thing, of course. And it is noted that Mr King no longer roams the streets of London in a car but resides in a luxurious Californian home that is owned by the society.

Meanwhile, the ground work is done by acolytes such as Mrs Henderson, who soon after the Risley encounter became embroiled in battles with the local council because certain residents did not take too kindly to the thought of Aetherian ceremonies (even weddings) taking place in a converted garage in downtown Warrington.

All that said, it is fascinating that one of the logged cases reported in the *Warrington Guardian* on that fateful day of 17 March was as follows: 'Four Warrington youngsters sighted a cigar-shaped object hovering over the United Kingdom Atomic Energy Authority Complex at Risley.'

This might give cause for wonder. Whilst it seems highly improbable that Ken Edwards imagined his story (even assuming he had a chance to read the local paper that day), it is possible that others claiming UFO sightings may have done. The Aetherius Society, of course, are naturally eager to endorse their religious message, and any number of UFO spotters could be out to show that their town is as good a place as Winsford any day. They had even been given the likely venue for where a UFO episode should take place – the Atomic Energy plant at Risley. By a marvel of coincidence, that is exactly where one *did* happen.

Of course, there is absolutely no evidence to show that any of these sources would either wish to, or did, perpetrate some sort of hoax that night in Daten Avenue. But the fascinating coincidence of that *Warrington Guardian* story on the very day in question seems too good to be true.

The Ken Edwards story quickly made national headlines, bolstered by the *Close Encounters* connection. Despite the fact that Ken never saw nor inferred any kind of UFO link himself, the media did. Not much more than twenty-four hours after the experience people were reading about it over breakfast. The *Sunday Post* proclaimed 'silvery giant beams light fantastic'. The *People* was more true to the UFO theme, heading its piece 'Close encounter as Ken meets a monster'. Perhaps the prize for the most inventive title of the lot should go to the *News of the World* with 'Ken and a flasher from outer space'.

As you can see, millions of people had been told that the strange white figure which Ken had encountered was a spaceman. In fact, he saw no UFO and the ghostly appearance and behaviour of the entity is far more typical of a spectral apparition than an alien. But the story was made to fit the UFO stereotype and an unstoppable wave of public interest was set in motion which poor Ken and Barbara Edwards, and the Padgate police, had simply not anticipated.

The story was a one-day wonder so far as the press were concerned. All the information they had was Ken's original description of the event to the police. In fact this meant that they missed some vital aspects of the case which only emerged in the cold light of our subsequent enquiries.

The time lapse, for example. This was something no newspaper picked up on in their haste to get a story into print. It only came to attention when we carefully reconstructed events with the witness. His suggestion as to why three-quarters of an hour was unaccounted for was that he must have sat in his car after the figure had vanished, paralysed with fear. Whilst this is possible, it seems unlikely. He had stopped in the middle of the road and was very much in the way of other traffic.

Time lapses such as this occur in what are called 'close encounters of the fourth kind' – one step beyond Steven Spielberg. It often takes the use of hypnosis, performed by qualified experts, to penetrate what is in effect a memory blackout. When this occurs, almost invariably an even more incredible tale of kidnap by strange beings tends to emerge.

Whether this might have happened in Ken Edwards's case will never be known. The suggestion was only put to him much later, when he was in a fit state to cope. He never believed that he was abducted by anything (or indeed that there was even a real chunk of missing time) and he was reluctant to submit himself to hypnosis. So the matter was not pursued. Our first report on this time anomaly did not appear until the end of 1978, but Ken says that in the weeks after the sighting he had several mysterious phone calls from strangers who seemed to know about it.

Four of these were described by Ken and Barbara when Jenny talked to them during 1979. One had come from a man with a Geordie accent who claimed to be a scientist working for NASA. On each occasion the callers asked Ken to be hypnotized, at their expense and with them making all arrangements. He said he needed time to think about this but the same person never called twice.

There were other weird calls during this first twelve months. One came from a man claiming to be a private detective who wanted to ask some searching questions. He ultimately revealed that a UFO investigator had put him on to Ken to try and prove that he was a liar.

However, oddest of all was a call from a man who said he worked as a presenter on a radio station in Birmingham. Could he come and interview Ken? By now, Ken and Barbara were thoroughly fed up with the whole affair and wished they had never reported it in the first place. So Ken said no. A few weeks later he had to go to Birmingham on business and, having changed his mind and feeling that he might have been a little harsh on the journalist, he called in at the radio station, BRMB. They had nobody on their staff of the name given to Ken. But even stranger than that – the name he had been given was George King, the same as the cab driver who (quite unknown to Ken Edwards) had formed the Aetherius Society. There is no evidence that it was the same man.

That was not the only other role played by the cult in this affair. They were in fact initially responsible for the sheer frustration felt by the Edwardses. After the Sunday press had carried the story, a veritable entourage from the Warrington Aetherius branch descended upon Ken and Barbara's modest semi-detached home in the midst of a quiet housing estate. They practically held a sermon on the doorstep and did not leave until the mild-mannered engineer invited them in. As Ken said to us soon after, 'I am not at all religious and this lot were going on about how I was chosen by God and extremely privileged to have seen this space being. I did not feel very privileged by the time they had finished, but I let them have their say just to get rid of them.'

What with this, crackpot literature that poured through their letter box, incessant calls from the world's press and then the more weird phone conversations, the couple were gradually driven to the point of despair. 'The last thing we would recommend anyone to do if they have an experience like this is talk about it,' Barbara said later. Their plans for a holiday were thrown into turmoil and in the end they simply had to get out of the house and visit relatives just to escape the constant pressure of living with a UFO experience.

UFO investigators from all over Britain flocked to see the Edwardses and they always tried to be accommodating. Michael Burt, who was with a group in Rochdale at the time, told us of several visits he and some colleagues paid to Risley. 'There was a particular area that Ken would not venture near. This seemed strange since it was not the scene of his encounter, but it was an area into which he claimed to have seen lights dropping.'

Michael Burt describes a dark night in mid-October 1978 when they met Ken in this place (known as 'the wood'). Ken made an excuse and left but they remained and encountered two strange glowing lights inside the dense tree cover as they bravely ventured down a path. Later Ken rejoined them and at just before midnight 'in the direction of Manchester Airport a large orange triangle appeared in the sky'. This pulsed, wavered about and changed shape, but as Ken desperately tried to focus his camera the button refused to depress. The golden-orange mass remained for several minutes before fading away and according to Michael Burt, 'it was actually below, or projected on to, cloud'.

This wooded area is said to provide nervous dispositions and illness in people who regularly visit it, according to Mr Burt. But we will have more to say on all this later, since the resolution may be illuminating.

In early April 1978, when things were quieter and it was possible to talk to the couple without such distractions, we learnt a good deal more about the aftermath of the encounter. For example, Ken's fingers were burnt on the inside. This effect, not dissimilar to sunburn, was on the right hand, affecting the little finger and the two fingers adjacent to it. Each mark was several inches long and, although Ken was very reluctant to attach any significance to them, both he and his wife were certain they had not existed prior to the sighting. They had not been abroad; they did not have a sunlamp and, needless to say, sunburn is not exactly feasible in England as early as mid-March.

It appeared that these burns were on the fingers which had been holding the steering wheel – the same ones exposed to the beams of light supposedly emitted from the strange figure's eyes. We both saw these burns and they were unquestionably real, although Ken had no history of skin ailments.

The thing about these burns which most amazed Jenny was that they paralleled exactly an image from the Spielberg movie. Neither Ken nor Barbara Edwards had then seen it. In the film Roy Nearey (played by actor Richard Dreyfuss) is hit by a beam from a UFO and finds that half his face turns brown overnight whilst the side that was in shadow does not. Although that scene was based on genuine cases of radiating

UFOs, such cases are rare and this kind of shadow effect rarer still. This coincidence was yet another weird feature of this case. But lest you think this was an invention on Ken's part to tie his story into the film, ask yourself why he never mentioned this to the press. Or indeed why the Edwardses never made a penny out of any of the media reports.

Another thing that emerged during the investigation was that Ken's watch had stopped at exactly 11.45 P.M., some minutes after he first saw the figure. Although it later began to work again, this offered hints about the possibility of something else having taken place during the period missing from his memory. His description of how he felt during this time is also enlightening: 'My head was swimming with strange thoughts. There were hundreds of them, all racing through my mind at once ... I also felt very odd. It was a sensation like two enormous hands pressing down on me from the top. The pressure was tremendous. It seemed to paralyse me. I could only move my eyes. The rest of me was rigid.'

Although there is no reason to believe that Ken Edwards knew this, it is a very common description given by people who have undergone similar close encounters. In January 1976, a young woman in Bolton had reported an identical effect during her sighting, and even spoke of pushing her umbrella into the ground to counteract the force. Ken also does not recall turning the engine off, or back on again. But there was no noticeable loss of petrol, which seems to imply that the engine may not have been idling for three-quarters of an hour.

Undoubtedly the most serious effect of the close encounter did not appear until the following Monday morning, when Ken next had to take his van to work. He tried to use the transceiver radio to call base and it failed to operate. It was looked over by electricians who could do nothing immediately and had to take it out for further study. The investigation report from the electricians was received just before Jenny's visit to the Edwardses. It was a real surprise. There had been an enormous power surge (probably through the aerial) which had burned out the entire transmitting diode circuit, practically with the force of an explosion. Most of the capacitators in the circuit were useless also. The cost of replacing the components was so high (over £200 estimated, at 1978 prices) that it was cheaper for the company to buy a new one, which is what they did.

A number of other things occurred in the days after the encounter, which yet again were missed by the reporters. On 23 March, six days after first seeing the entity, Ken says that he met a UFO investigator from Leeds. He took the man to the site and began to feel very dizzy. Once more he saw, out of the corner of his eye, what he believes was the same figure. It was there for just a few moments.

On 2 April Ken and Barbara returned from a day out in Yorkshire. It was 2 A.M. as they turned off the slip road on to Daten Avenue and passed the location of the encounter. Ken says that he felt an urge to stop and get out of the car. Despite protests from his wife he stood there, staring blankly into space for a few moments, until she dragged him back in and made him drive home. He believes he lost consciousness for a few seconds. From that day on he declined to take this short cut, preferring to join the motorway on the Newton-Le-Willows road, despite this involving a lengthy detour.

All of these repercussions in the wake of the initial sighting suggest things which might be important. However, the saddest and perhaps most important fact of all is that Ken is no longer with us to tell his story.

During one of her routine check-up calls to Ken Edwards in mid-1982, Jenny was shocked to hear Barbara report that he had died. He was only forty-two, but any connection between this untimely demise and the 1978 encounter is circumstantial . . .

Ken himself never connected his illness with the experience. But Barbara did point out that one could not be so certain. A thing which can burn skin, stop watches and destroy an expensive radio transmitter might well be capable of bringing harm to a human being.

Ken's illness followed this course: less than a year after the encounter he began to feel unusually tired and suffer stomach cramps. He visited his doctor who sent him to a specialist, where cancer of the kidneys was diagnosed. In early 1980 he underwent major surgery, which it was hoped might catch the disease before it spread. This seemed to work. However, within a few months cancer of the throat developed and despite treatment and a further operation it was beyond control. Ken lost his brave fight just under four years after the meeting with that fateful glowing object on Daten Avenue.

Let us now try to piece together what might have been responsible for Ken's terrifying ordeal. It is worth first taking a closer look at the area where the entity appeared. Today Daten Avenue is not exactly a busy main road, particularly at night, but it does have traffic. The exit from the M62 motorway now serves Birchwood, a major new town development with over 20,000 inhabitants, which has grown out of nothing since 1979. Gorse Covert is the estate nearest to the site, although it was the last to be built and did not exist in any form in 1978. It now contains the large expanse of peat bog and woodland known as Risley Moss which is a fully staffed nature reserve with visitors' facilities providing sanctuary for various kinds of bird and animal life. This is, in fact, the wood referred to previously by Michael Burt, where Ken allegedly saw his regular 'lights' and where he and the group encountered the orange triangle.

This is about half a mile from the spot where Ken met the entity. In between Daten Avenue and the nature reserve is a depot owned by the AA which houses Relay vehicles. This is where Ken saw the entity on the second occasion, just a hundred yards or so along Daten Avenue from the fateful spot of his closer encounter.

Risley itself is a very small place, comprising little more than a few houses, a golf course and the infamous 'Risley Remand Centre – a holding prison for people awaiting trial. It has the nickname Grisly Risley because crowding is so intense and the number of inmates who hang themselves in their cells has at times been considered alarming. The remand centre is on the northern side of the motorway from Daten Avenue, about one mile away.

Whilst the development of new housing at Birchwood has now swallowed Risley, the area was still very countrified in 1978. By coincidence, Jenny Randles moved there during early 1980, and she came to know the Risley Moss nature reserve very well. Many lights in the sky were indeed visible to the south, but they were simply aircraft heading into Manchester Airport. Although about twelve miles from the airport, Risley acts as a holding zone for some flights. Aircraft lights can frequently be seen on clear nights. As the airport is one of the busiest in Europe, especially during the summer, anyone unfamiliar with the area might consider this odd.

Additionally, the peat causes the ground to be exceptionally springy (a bit like a mattress in places). It absorbs water and can lead to marsh gas and other natural phenomena inside the woodland.

Finally, the 'orange triangle' certainly exists. Jenny saw it herself on many occasions. It is produced by burn-off from the huge Shell oil refinery at Carrington, about seven miles south. Normally this is dimly visible as a tiny flame if you look closely at the right spot. However, on nights when the cloud base is low the flames reflect off it spectacularly to create a quite colourful display that has fooled a number of people who are merely passing through.

In other words, none of the facts of the alleged secondary sightings by Ken Edwards and these UFO investigators are

ᴏᴠᴇ: Frederick Valentich,
ᴛ of the 'flight into
ivion'
rtesy UFO INFO)

ʜᴛ: Carol Compton talks
ᴇr mother from behind
s at the opening of her
l
rtesy Associated Press)

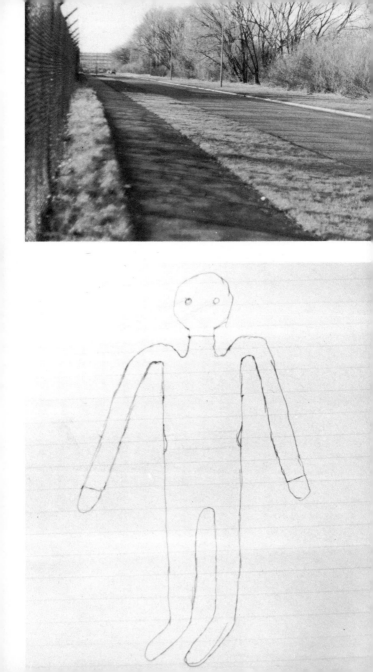

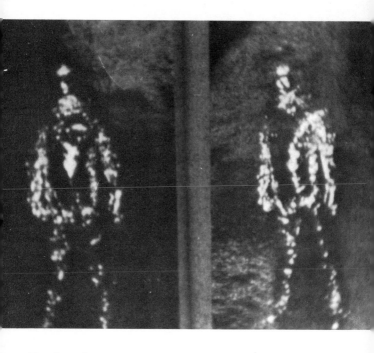

ABOVE: Two shots of an
alleged alien entity in a silver
suit taken by Police Officer
Jeff Greenhaw in Falkville,
Alabama. The entity is very
similar to that reported by
Ken Edwards

ABOVE LEFT: Daten Avenue,
Risley, Cheshire. Scene of
Ken Edwards' encounter
with the 'spectre of death'

BELOW LEFT: Ken Edwards'
original sketch of the figure
he saw

LEFT: Jacqueline Fitzsimon
(*courtesy Stuart Bogg*)

BELOW: Halton College of
Further Education, where
Jacqueline Fitzsimon was
studying to be a cook

ABOVE: West Yorkshire
Police Officer Alan Godfrey,
at the location of his strange
encounter in Todmordern

RIGHT: Alan Godfrey's boot,
showing the damage he
discovered after his
encounter

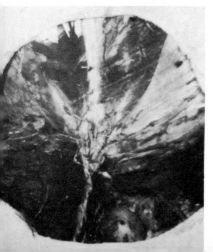

ABOVE: Mutilated cow from Van Zandt County, Texas
(courtesy Grand Saline Police Dept)

LEFT: Close-up showing where vital organs have been surgically removed
(courtesy Grand Saline Police Dept)

The grave of William 'Noble'
Edden, murdered in 1828, in
Thame churchyard
(*courtesy Alan Cleaver*)

in question, all of them having perfectly rational explanations.

The entire Birchwood and Risley area is built atop what was once a huge munitions dump during the last war. Some of the old concrete storage bunkers still exist and have been landscaped over to form a park. The Ministry of Supply took over the Ordnance Factory on 6 February 1947 and quickly saw the potential for developing the site into a centre for the UK Atomic Energy Authority (UKAEA). This was created in 1954 and the buildings modernized and expanded to produce a very large complex of offices and research laboratories. However, there is no reactor on the site and, as public relations officer Sandy Gregg was very insistent in pointing out to us, 'There is no radioactivity here.'

A ten-foot-high security fence straddles the length of Daten Avenue on the south side, protecting the UKAEA site. A grass embankment beyond the fence acts as another deterrent to potential trespassers. Checks of the fencing were made by the police less than three hours after Ken's sighting. It was checked the next morning in daylight by the UKAEA staff. Both authors independently checked it with Ken Edwards before mid-April 1978. All of these investigations found no sign of even the most minute hole and there was absolutely no way that any normal figure could have passed through the fence into the grounds of the atomic energy plant, or indeed climbed over the fence without considerable difficulty. Jenny Randles also tried emulating the manner in which the figure allegedly walked down the grass embankment on the north side of the road, under Ken's directions. This proved virtually impossible, due to steepness and heavy brambles, and required great caution and a backwards lean.

Despite these things Ken remained totally convinced that the figure had walked down bending forward and then passed straight through the security fence, climbed the embankment inside the complex and disappeared. If these statements are correct, then even without reference to any of the other physical evidence, they rule out any practical possibility of a conventional solution.

However, the idea that the figure in the suit was someone very terrestrial was of course the most important thing which the Padgate police had to consider. This is why they drove back with the still distraught witness and spent several hours on site with the night security staff at the UKAEA.

In August 1987 Jenny spoke to PC Bob Thomson, the New Town Liaison Officer who looked after Risley. He remembered the case well. 'Locally it was treated as a bit of a joke, but that man was under a lot of pressure. We can't treat these things as jokes, of course. We have to investigate them. But there isn't a lot we can do, really.'

Another officer, now retired, but who was involved at the time, is Roy Kirkpatrick. He actually lives in the same road as the Edwards family. He knew them both. Kirkpatrick told Jenny, 'It was taken seriously back then. The man was frightened. He'd obviously seen something strange. We thought at the time it was a fireman – because the old fire hut for the UKAEA is just opposite. It's now bricked up, but firemen in radiation suits could once have walked past that spot across the road.'

Perhaps you are wondering why, if as the UKAEA insist there is no radiation on site, firemen wear radiation suits at Risley. The answer to that will emerge in a moment, but you can presumably see why the police were so willing to believe this idea. They considered that Ken Edwards' fear was real. He *had* seen something. If that something had been a fireman clambering down the embankment at such a late hour, his silver foil suit shining in the headlights, it would be enough to frighten anyone.

However, when the police arrived at the UKAEA early that Saturday morning the plant was quiet and no firemen in uniform were on duty or had been there at 11.30 P.M.

Sandy Gregg at the UKAEA kindly checked the records

for us and said, 'Obviously, had it been one of our people messing around, it would have been serious. It would have been even more serious if there had been a security intrusion. Once we had satisfied ourselves it was not – and that it could not have been one of our suits – then it was up to the police. According to their reports, the people who were on duty that night say the man [Ken Edwards] was scared. He'd seen something.'

Ken would need to have been a superb actor to have convinced all these people of his sincerity and terror, or to have kept it up for so long, unless he really had met something 'out of this world'. But in order to convince themselves, both the Padgate police and the UKAEA staff arranged a little subterfuge. As daylight broke on the Saturday morning, two officers called for Ken and asked him to come back with them to the plant for further questions. As they drove into the complex a fireman dressed in full radiation gear stepped from the side of the building at a prearranged signal right into the path of the patrol car.

Instantly one police officer turned to the witness and said, 'That's what you saw – wasn't it?'

He did not bat an eyelid and gazed back at them both implacably, the memory of his encounter less than twelve hours before still etched into his mind. 'Nope! Nothing like it,' he told them.

As far as both the police and the UKAEA were concerned that was all they could do. It was not a man in a fire suit.

In 1981, David Forster from Widnes published a letter in Issue 27 of the Orbis partwork *The Unexplained*. He claimed to be employed at the UKAEA plant and raised (he thought for the first time) the issue of the fire suits. He said that 'discreet enquiries' had produced the startling news that it was a rag stunt carried out by Padgate College (now North Cheshire College of Higher Education).

Although the college is over a mile from Daten Avenue (on

the western side of the M6 motorway) it is closer to where the Edwards family live. It is hard to conceive how such a stunt might be pulled off and, more importantly, why nobody owned up to it: the point of stunts is to achieve publicity. However, this might fit the scenario of someone having read the *Warrington Guardian* story that day and noted that the UKAEA plant was the place to see UFOs in the town.

It has not proved possible to verify Forster's theory. Despite his claim that a student had confessed to the trick, the student never did so to Ken, although he publicly asked the student to admit to it. As he said when Jenny discussed the student hoax solution with him, 'I wish he or she would come forward and tell me how they did it . . . How they blew up my radio and walked through the fence. It was some stunt!'

Enquiries at the college have utterly failed to vindicate this claim. It appears to have been an unfounded rumour and nothing more. The UKAEA had checked it. Sandy Gregg told us, 'It was not a rag stunt. It was too early in the year anyway.' Police officer Bob Thomson confirmed that. 'Nothing ever came of our enquiries into that.'

However, his ex-colleague Roy Kirkpatrick was more open-minded. 'The college did get up to silly stunts back then, you know, stealing wheels from cars and so on. I caught someone once taking a security board away from the old armaments place. But we looked into the idea. There was no rag on at the time and nobody ever admitted it. We never could find evidence for such a link.'

So it would appear that all options for a conventional answer do not lead very far. What about unconventional options?

Sandy Gregg has studied the history of the area. Risley was founded by Thomas Risley, and the church he built is one of the oldest Presbyterian buildings in England. When the M62 scythed through the Cheshire landscape the church itself was demolished, but the graveyard remains – only a few hundred yards from Daten Avenue. The restless spirits of the Risleys may well be unhappy about what the twentieth century has done to their village. Once a sleepy spot, it has had to suffer the roar of traffic, the horrible emotional strains of the remand centre, the fears and tensions produced by the huge armaments dumps, and now the take-over by nuclear research. If the Earth itself had any say in how it is used one might imagine a revolt beginning at Risley.

If we were forced to consider the idea of a ghost being responsible for the apparition on Daten Avenue, it is possible that a fireman coming back to haunt the site might be a candidate. However, there is no record of any fire officer having died there.

The old fire station, which Roy Kirkpatrick referred to, was located on the far side of Daten Avenue from the plant for a good reason. It is also the reason why the staff have radiation suits. There *is* a reactor, but it is not part of the UKAEA complex. It is a 'research reactor' on a small scale that is owned and operated by Liverpool and Manchester universities. As the scientists here explained, 'We do not have any firemen. We use Atomic Energy Authority fire staff.'

It was not easy to make any discoveries about the work that goes on here. Nobody at Manchester University admitted to knowledge about it. We tried Liverpool and ultimately made progress through rather cagey staff at Clatterbridge Hospital on the Wirral. This, interestingly enough, is one of the country's leading cancer research units.

The university research building has another rather odd function. It conducts experiments into sensory deprivation. As far as we could ascertain from the police (again the universities were reluctant to talk) people are locked in a small room for days on end and denied all normal stimuli and thus the way human beings react to prolonged isolation can be investigated.

Roy Kirkpatrick spoke of this Isolation Unit, as it is called.

'It was in use back in 1978. Cars often parked in the lay-by right next to where Ken saw the entity, as the building is just at the top of the embankment where he said the figure came from. I remember once passing one woman who was parked there late at night. I drove past again in the early hours of the morning and she was still there. She told me that she was giving her husband moral support, as he was locked inside and she wanted to wait until he was released because he might be disorientated.'

Those of an imaginative frame of mind might ponder the fact that hallucinations of glowing white lights and figures are commonly reported during isolation. For example, an account of sessions carried out on himself in an isolation tank can be found in Dr John Lilly's bizarre but thought-provoking book *The Centre of the Cyclone* (Calder and Boyars, 1973). He refers to his belief, based on extensive research and experimentation, that these glowing beings are in a dimension of inner space. Whether they are contacted, evoked like demons or created by the mind is almost irrelevant to him. He also says he shared telepathic experiences with others in similar states of sensory deprivation.

It might be interesting to speculate about someone in the unit who was possibly hallucinating or dreaming just as Ken Edwards happened to drive past. Ken was concluding a long, quiet drive and might conceivably be in the sort of state of consciousness that would enable him to 'tune in' to the sensory deprivation victim's nightmare.

Of course, this is a theory on the edge of plausibility. And it also does little to explain the very real physical effects on the car radio transmitter, the watch or Ken's fingers.

Unfortunately it was not possible to get much help from the research unit itself. Indeed, Jenny was told quite abruptly, 'Why revive interest in this matter now?' The scientists there appeared more suspicious and reluctant to talk than anybody else in this entire enquiry. People were generally as intrigued and puzzled as anyone should be by Ken Edwards's story. Yet the person at the Isolation Unit would not even give a name. The most they would say, clearly with little enthusiasm, was, 'The story going round is that it was one of the Atomic Energy firemen acting stupid.' As you have seen it is quite certain this was not the case.

So, could the figure really have been from a UFO? Who can say? There had been a spate of UFO entity sightings in early 1978 (well before the Spielberg movie arrived). These concentrated in Cheshire and Merseyside, including two in January. Oddly, both had involved a group of four young men – in the first case at Rainford, about eighteen miles west of Risley, and the second, three weeks later, at Frodsham, about twelve miles southwest.

The Rainford entity was seen without any UFO being present, making it very similar to the Risley case. One of the men became so terrified that an asthma attack was induced. The police were called out to investigate that event also, but could find no explanation, although one intrepid UFO investigator, Dr Robert Morrell from Nottingham, later suggested that they had merely run into a stray cow that had wandered on to the road and been caught in the headlights of the vehicle.

Funnily enough, cows featured in the Frodsham story too. Here the four men (including the son of a local dignitary) were poaching in fields by the River Weaver when, they claimed, a spherical object landed and some silver-suited figures emerged and placed a cage-like piece of equipment on to apparently immobilized cows. Fearing that they might be next in line, they fled in terror.

However, despite all this (and another impressive sighting by motorway patrol police on the M62 west of Warrington), there were no reports of UFOs being seen at the same time and place as Ken Edwards met that figure on Daten Avenue.

Nevertheless, there was what might be termed a mini-wave

of events peaking late that Friday night. No less than eight other cases are on the records of the Northern UFO Network for the period from late afternoon on 17 March to exactly twenty-four hours after Ken's encounter. This is ten times the average. Since there are in fact just 284 sightings for the entire year throughout the northern counties covered by the network, eight happening in just thirty hours is seen to be highly significant, even more so because there was no possibility that Ken could have known about this on 17 March. Most of the sightings did not receive any publicity at all. Six of these eight sightings were scattered between 7 P.M. on the 17th and 3 A.M. on the 18th, placing Ken's right in the middle. It certainly appears to demonstrate that there was very intense and unusual UFO activity that night.

In the end we *are* left with a mystery, but the evidence that links it with UFOs (as the media so rapidly announced) is circumstantial. Indeed, most of the important detail was unknown to the reporters who conjured up the headlines that Sunday morning. Had they known of the effects on the radio, or the previous entity sightings in the area, or the major wave of sightings that day, they might have been justified in their claim. As it was, they appear to have wanted little more than to foster a topical myth.

We can only ponder all the options. Meanwhile, Bob Thomson tells us, 'I know the family. Ken wasn't a drinker. It was quite strange.' Roy Kirkpatrick says, 'I wish we could find out what happened. That man was really scared. Something odd *did* take place!'

4

A Case of Spontaneous Human Confusion

Monday 28 January 1985; a chill, unsettled day. The students filed into Halton College of Further Education charging the corridors with noise, the clip-clop of stilettos, curses and laughter. It was good to be out of the cold, but the weekend was gone now, and several days of work loomed ahead.

Like many of the students, Jacqueline Fitzsimon was on the Youth Training Scheme. She was studying to be a cook. That morning the class was to be different. A practical examination had been arranged.

Jacqueline, dark-haired and attractive, entered Room C16 with two of her friends just before 9 A.M. Although the cookery room possessed radiators, to save money they were rarely turned on. The ambient heat from the cookers was supposed to be sufficient. This morning Mr Carson, their tutor, had already lit the ovens well in advance. Jacqueline stood with her friends, Wendy Hughes and Paula McGeever. There were six other students, all chatting amicably until Carson called them to order.

Robert Carson was in his mid-forties, stocky, with fair hair flecked with grey. He had a mouth which stretched from ear to ear, the sort of mouth which always seemed to be smiling. He was grinning now as he explained to the class exactly what the examination entailed.

It was straightforward enough. There were three things to be prepared: crème caramel, sponge pudding and bread rolls. The students paired off, Jacqueline sharing a cooker with Wendy, and the exam began.

By 9.40, Carson noticed with satisfaction that all the class had completed the crème caramel. At this stage, the rings on the cookers should have been turned off, as they were no longer required. An hour later, ahead of the others, Jacqueline and Wendy, together with Paula, had completed the entire exam. There was a scheduled break at 11 A.M., but rather than hang around, Jacqueline asked if they could leave early.

'I'm sorry, girls,' Carson said, 'but the answer is no. This is an exam. You'll have to wait until everyone is finished.'

They were not happy with this reply, but they knew it was a waste of time arguing with him. Instead they whiled away the time leaning against the worktops, chatting about music, boyfriends and television. As the clock edged towards eleven, the three girls moved over to the doorway in readiness to leave. As they would be returning after the break, they kept on the white smocks they'd worn during cooking.

In the meantime, another lecturer entered the room, and he and Carson watched the girls, passing a few comments. During this time, neither of the men noticed anything odd about Jacqueline's clothing. Just before eleven o'clock, Carson dismissed the class.

The girls were in high spirits as they made their way through the building towards the canteen. Linking arms, singing, they were normal happy teenagers. Certainly no one passing them along the corridors noticed anything unusual.

At that time, two mature students, John Foy and Neil Gargan, were heading in the opposite direction. They were walking up the stairs between 'B' and 'C' floors when they saw the girls talking animatedly. As they passed, neither of the men saw smoke or smelt burning.

Close by, three staff members were in conference in one of the offices: student director James Witton, lecturer Alan Harmer, and senior lecturer Edward Davies.

By now the girls had unlinked arms and Wendy Hughes started to go on ahead down the steps towards 'B' floor. She had just reached the bottom when this dull, winter's day took on the proportions of a nightmare. Jacqueline's voice suddenly echoed down the stairwell, rising as terror took hold.

'My back's gone hot!' she cried out. 'What's happening? Am I on fire? I'm on fire! I'm on fire!'

Just a few moments had passed since John and Neil had walked by; now, hearing the teenager's screams, they raced back, realizing something was terribly wrong. Yet they were totally unprepared for what they saw.

One of the girls they had just seen was panic stricken, shouting, her back sprouting flames as convincingly as a television stunt man. She danced around hysterically, holding her lacquered hair high above her head with one hand, reaching uselessly behind her with the other. Smouldering pieces of cloth were rising into the air as the two men made a grab for her.

Hearing the commotion, James Witton and his colleagues burst out into the corridor and saw Jacqueline at the bottom of the stairs, struggling to tear off her disintegrating smock. With the aid of John Foy's jacket, the flames were finally smothered. She lay where she had finally fallen, on the floor, while an ambulance was called.

All this time she was fully conscious, her weeping friend, Paula, trying to comfort her. Curiously, Jacqueline seemed oblivious to any pain in her back, but complained about a finger injured while she was trying to rip off her smock. Underneath was an acrylic jumper which had melted and clung to her skin.

During the four-mile ride to Whiston Hospital, accompanied by her friend, Jacqueline remained rational throughout. There she was kept in intensive care for several days, suffering from superficial burns to her body, including buttocks and back, from bra to panty line. It was not until two days after the incident, on 30 January, that the police were informed.

Detective Sergeant Abel and Detective Constable Plant of

the CID visited the college at 6 P.M. that night to find the place rife with rumours. DS Abel, in his late thirties, tall with dark hair, was an experienced officer used to dealing with hardened criminals. It should have been easy to get to the bottom of this little mystery. Just how did Jacqueline Fitzsimon's back become a mass of flames, when moments earlier there was nothing? An interview with the victim might throw light on the matter, DS Abel conjectured, although things which appeared simple on the surface had a habit of turning out complicated.

The officers were immediately impressed by Jacqueline's outgoing personality, evident despite the pain of her injuries. They arrived at the hospital after having taken statements at Halton College, and talked to Jackie in the company of her father. Mr Fitzsimon sat close by. He had a very erect, stocky figure, and wore his hair swept back. There was an inner strength abundantly obvious in the man, which was to prove a boon for his wife in the coming months.

Jacqueline was sitting up in bed, positive, and in the circumstances quite happy, DS Abel was to lament later. He questioned her closely regarding the circumstances leading up to the fire, then said, 'Jacqueline, how do *you* think it happened?'

She pulled a face. 'I suppose at some point I must have been leaning against the cooker. That's the only thing which makes sense, isn't it?'

'You mean the ring was still lit, even though you had finished?'

'Yeah, it was cold in there.'

'And you were definitely leaning against it?'

'Can't say for sure . . .'

Although it still seemed a *likely* explanation, the officers were not happy with this. It seemed like an easy option which ignored most of the peripheral facts. After all, the girl only *thought* she might have been leaning against the cooker. She had no clear memory of having done so.

Jacqueline's testimony lost its value further when the Detective Sergeant discovered she had already discussed the possible explanations with several of her friends. Wendy Hughes had certainly repeated all the stories circulating around college. Abel knew that by the time the police had been drawn into it, Jacqueline had already made up her mind. But in truth, the pretty teenager was as much in the dark as anyone else.

One of the rumours which was to gain prominence and make the incident national headline material concerned the alleged phenomenon of Spontaneous Human Combustion. There are documented cases from around the world of people who, for no apparent reason, have inexplicably burst into flames. Most, although not all, have been reduced to a heap of fine ash, leaving the surrounding area relatively untouched. Had Jacqueline Fitzsimon become a victim of SHC?

The girl herself obviously did not know. The only certainty in her mind was that several minutes after leaving Room C16, her back became a writhing mass of flames.

Suddenly, tragedy heaped itself on tragedy. Unexpectedly, Jackie took a turn for the worse. At 5.34 P.M. on 12 February she died.

INVESTIGATION

Spontaneous Human Combustion is a rare phenomenon that strikes instantly, hungrily bringing about injury and death in a most bizarre and cruel manner. Fire from nowhere.

Reports of the phenomenon, although not 'officially' recognized, go back a very long way. SHC was popularized during the last century by Charles Dickens, who based the macabre death of his character Krook, in *Bleak House*, on genuine accounts. Dickens was severely criticized for it at the time.

On 5 January 1835 Mr James Hamilton, Professor of Mathematics at Nashville University, was walking home in the intense cold, according to Dr John Overton writing in the *Transactions of the Medical Society of Tennessee*. While checking the hygrometer hanging outside his house, Hamilton felt 'a steady pain like a hornet sting, accompanied by a sensation of heat' in his left leg. Looking down he 'distinctly saw a light flame of the extent ... of a ten cent piece ... having a complexion which nearest resembles that of pure quicksilver'.

Instinctively the professor slapped at the flame but to no avail. In some pain, he still managed to bring cool scientific methods into practice, and cupped his hands around the area to cut off the oxygen. The fire extinguished itself. The fortunate man survived the flame, which Dr Overton claimed, after treating Hamilton, had started *internally*.

Almost exactly a hundred and fifty years later, the fire struck down teenager Jacqueline Fitzsimon, this time with fatal consequences. Or did it? Was there a more mundane explanation?

The British media were not long in taking advantage of the confusion and in fuelling the flames of the SHC rumours. According to the *Daily Express* of 25 February, in an item headed 'College In Quiz Over Girl Who Died In Flames': 'The heartbroken parents of a seventeen-year-old girl who suddenly burst into flames said yesterday: "Our daughter's death is a complete mystery. No one seems to know what happened." Pretty Jacqueline Fitzsimon is believed to have been a victim of Spontaneous Human Combustion. Forensic experts investigating Jacqueline's death said yesterday: "It is a real possibility at the moment. We cannot find any other reason, but the investigation is still going on." The North Merseyside coroner has now ordered a full investigation. Seven eye witnesses have made statements, and reports are being prepared by police, fire chiefs and the Government's Health and Safety Executive.'

The *Daily Express* article was just one account among a number of other newspaper and television features in the wake of the original and quickly adjourned inquest of 22 February. At this, Cheshire Fire Prevention Officer Bert Gilles was reputed to have said: 'I have interviewed seven eye witnesses. So far there is no clear explanation of the fire . . . we must look for other causes like Spontaneous Human Combustion. Spontaneous Human Combustion is a theory most of us have previously treated highly sceptically, but it should be examined.'

The authorities and various governmental 'experts' took the next four months to make their enquiries and carry out what scientific analysis was necessary to discover the cause of a fire which seemed to come from nowhere, and turn a pretty teenage girl into 'a television stunt man'.

During this same time, Larry Arnold, a noted SHC investigator in the United States, spent considerable time and money making telephone enquiries over here. In a letter to Peter Hough, Arnold remarked that the coroner had bluntly told him, 'You are wasting your time pursuing this.' The American pointed out to Hough that this was in March, and at the start of the investigation; yet even at this stage the coroner had judged that SHC was not involved.

Arnold cites a similar attitude in his own country towards the phenomenon. He calls it 'a conspiracy of confusion'. The authorities cannot explain it, so they act as if it does not exist.

As paranormal investigators we were intrigued to find a case with such strong SHC overtones, but we knew that we were dealing with a very human tragedy, and we decided to tread carefully in the subsequent investigation we were planning. All we wanted to do was get to the bottom of the mystery. For all the talk about SHC it was far from clear what exactly had occurred.

The cookery connection seemed suspect, and although the Fire Prevention Officer had made reference to SHC, there were a number of atypical features contrary to the bulk of other reports. No mention had been made of the unusual bluish flame said to consume victims. Also Jacqueline had not been virtually incinerated or turned to ash (the predominant, although not the universal pattern), but had suffered relatively minor burns to her back, and had survived for over two weeks.

In order to begin enquiries Peter Hough wrote to the local CID and the principal of Halton College. There was no immediate response from the police, but the principal, in a letter dated 18 March, explained, 'Since a coroner's enquiry is due in the next few weeks I am unable to discuss the incident in any detail.'

Principal L. A. Hough (no relation) added that because of this it would be 'inappropriate' for us to be 'allowed to speak to the witnesses'.

The next move was a gentle approach to a local newspaper, the *Widnes Weekly World*. Although prohibited from making journalistic enquiries until after the inquest, their editor did agree to carry an interview with Peter Hough, in which he appealed for witnesses to contact him directly.

Great care was taken over what was said. The story, entitled 'Probe Into Mystery Death Of Student', appeared on 24 May. The address and telephone number of the investigator were included for contact. But the phone remained silent until twelve days later.

A man who would only identify himself as 'Brian' telephoned one night. Having been working away for the last two weeks, he had only just seen the article. Brian explained he had some inside information about the girl's death, and possessed 'something you might be interested to see'.

Peter Hough agreed to meet Brian in a quiet pub called the Cuerdley Cross, just outside Widnes, the following evening at 7.30 P.M. Although retaining his anonymity, Brian did allude to connections with the police and Whiston

Hospital. True to his word, he demonstrated his sincerity by producing objective evidence which seemed to indicate that Jacqueline had not been seriously burned. This suggested that, if SHC was involved, then its effects had been of a mild or partial nature. He also made a statement totally disputing the media claims of fifteen days' intensive care. He claimed that, just a few days after the fire, Jacqueline had been sitting up in bed, wearing make-up, talking cheerfully to friends and relatives. Her subsequent death looked more mysterious than before.

A few days later, Peter Hough arrived home to discover that two uniformed police officers from Greater Manchester had called and left a note, presumably as a result of his letter to the Cheshire CID (*not* his local force). It gave details of the date, time and place of the inquest, and ended with the ambiguous words: 'Please Attend'. Was this a suggestion or a request?

Clutching our police invitation we arrived to attend the inquest, held at council offices near Whiston Hospital, on 28 June – five months to the day after the student had burst into flames.

Naturally, we were expecting great things. After all, the official enquiry had now lasted several months, with fire officers, government departments and the police involved. But we saw no scientific and polished presentation of the facts. Instead, in our view, we were given a demonstration of weak investigation and little effort to resolve confusions.

When we entered the chambers the room was already filling. Witnesses were everywhere, and the six-member jury had documents and diagrams before them. At no time, despite requests, were we allowed to see this evidence close to.

As soon as we entered and stated our names, the man at the door, whom we took to be the court usher, clearly made us unwelcome. We were made to stand with the press at the back of the room, and over an hour elapsed before we were given permission to sit down.

A pathologist, Dr Cradwell, was the first to give evidence. He explained, in a little over two minutes, that he had carried out a post-mortem on 14 February. The girl had superficial external burns on her buttocks and back, from bra to panty line. Approximately 13 per cent burns were attested, which coincided closely with the evidence 'Brian' had earlier provided for Peter Hough. A brief discussion of damage to the lungs, including inflamed bronchial tubes, and septicaemia, followed. Death was due to 'shock-lung'.

We were listening intently, endeavouring to learn why Jacqueline had been so well a few days after the tragedy, and yet had subsequently died. We presumed cross-examination would elucidate this puzzle. Three solicitors were ranged opposite the jury, and all nine people had this right of cross-examination. The three legal men appeared to represent the family of the deceased, Halton College, and the authorities.

Throughout the inquest, these nine people frequently, sometimes tediously, availed themselves of this right. But Dr Cradwell – whose evidence was pivotal to the whole case – was never asked a single question! After finishing his hurried presentation he picked up his briefcase and immediately left the room. Perhaps the jury felt intimidated by the proceedings; certainly there were a lot of loose ends which they failed to pick up on.

We then learnt what had occurred during the cookery class. There were several contradictions about this, but the biggest mystery concerned the fifteen minutes from when Jacqueline Fitzsimon finished cooking to the time the class was dismissed. What had she been doing during this time?

Wendy Hughes and Paula McGeever gave evidence first. Both agreed that the three of them left the room ahead of the others, in high spirits, and none of them were smoking. The cooker rings, however, were *not* switched off after the caramel was made, because the room was cold and the cookers served as heating. Lecturer Robert Carson later vehemently denied this, although other staff pointed out that room C16 did not use radiators because it was naturally heated by the ovens.

Wendy and Paula suggested that the three of them had spent most of the unoccupied time leaning against the worktops and cookers, and that Jacqueline must have been about eight inches from the nearest lighted jet. However, they said that upon leaving the room none of them smelt or saw smouldering on their friend's back. Neither Carson nor his colleague, who also watched them leave, noticed anything either. The girls wore standard-issue white smocks, where burning would have been obvious.

Arms linked, they walked along the corridor to the top of the stairs, where Wendy unlinked and began moving down towards 'B' floor and the canteen. Both girls agreed that Jacqueline called out, 'My back's hot ... am I on fire?' Smouldering pieces of cloth were suddenly rising into the air, and inside a few seconds their friend was covered in flames.

Jacqueline finally collapsed in the corridor at the foot of the stairs. The girls, together with staff and other students, beat out the flames. An ambulance arrived and took her to Whiston Hospital, where she remained conscious and lucid throughout.

The statements offered by these two witnesses left us wondering. They offered a simple, if unhappy explanation. The flame from the gas ring had set Jacqueline's smock smouldering, later to burst into flames. But how did this smouldering go undetected for at least five minutes? Apart from the curious lack of smell and sight of this supposed smouldering, Jacqueline herself experienced no sensation of heat.

Two other students in the class next gave evidence, adding further to the confusion. Jamie Hayes insisted that the girls had been hanging around the door at least two minutes prior to leaving, adding to the smouldering time. Graham Littler was presented with a signed statement made to the Fire Officer on 29 January, the day after the tragedy, in which he said Paula McGeever told him she and Jacqueline had been in the toilets on 'C' floor before going down the stairs. Jacqueline had come out saying, 'I'm sure I'm on fire, can you smell burning?'

Previously both girls had flatly denied going into the toilets. Littler, although agreeing he had written the statement, now retracted it, and looked decidedly uncomfortable about the whole thing. The issue was not resolved.

Now, one of the solicitors advised us, there was a second theory. Had the girls been in the toilets playing 'flame-throwers' by lighting hairspray jets with matches? This insane game was seriously mooted to explain how Jacqueline had sprouted into flame so rapidly. Presumably, we thought, the forensic tests would clear up this matter, but we were much too optimistic.

Three more students from the class remained to give evidence. Marie Green claimed she had gone looking for Jacqueline after word got back to C16 of the incident. For some reason she went into the toilets, where the door was ajar, and found it full of smoke, with a smell of burned paper. In her statement, made after the day of the fire, she said a girl from the hairdressing class had told her, 'Your mate's just come out of the toilets on fire.' That was the reason she had made straight for the toilets.

Vanessa Dean confirmed all this, and had also seen the smoke. She also added that Jacqueline had been standing by the door, and well away from the cooker, for at least five minutes before leaving.

The latent smouldering theory was now in retreat, but had the SHC claims any foundation, and why, in some respects, was there such inconsistency amongst the witnesses? Both of these girls had mentioned Karen Quirk, another cookery student, who seemed to know something more about this rumour of Jacqueline running from the toilets. We settled back and waited for her to resolve the matter.

Despite being instructed to attend, it transpired that Karen had not turned up. Now an act of expediency was displayed by the inquest. Coroner Gordon Glasgow pointed out to both jury and solicitors that if any of them insisted on questioning Karen, then the inquest would have to be adjourned. Imagine our surprise when they all said that none of them wished to cross-examine the girl.

Two months after the inquest we called Karen Quirk but discovered from a disgruntled lady that the number had been changed and she was fed up with calls for Ms Quirk. She had been given the number in June and, despite being ex-directory, had received so many calls that the operator had tapped the line to intercept callers. We found Karen's new number through Directory Enquiries. Karen spoke reluctantly and briefly. Like many of the witnesses at the inquest she was uneasy and refused to make any comment on Spontaneous Human Combustion, although admitting that she had been questioned about it by fire officers. Neither would she be drawn on any other aspects of the case. She claimed that she had become lost on the day of the inquest, and stated that no one had enquired since why she had failed to attend.

Karen claimed her number had been changed because the family kept getting calls for a taxi firm. We found no evidence for this. In fact the closest match to a local taxi company we traced was for the Quirk's new number.

Back at the inquest, we next heard from two mature students, John Foy and Neil Gargan – HNC students in Electrical Engineering. They were totally objective witnesses in the sense that they neither knew nor had connections with anyone involved. We put great store by their cool and rational accounts, and it was from them that the SHC scenario at last found some support.

Foy works for Chloride Silent Power Ltd and Gargan for the Mersey Docks and Harbour Board. They were seconded part-time to the college. Both were walking up the stairs when they passed the three girls talking animatedly. Just a few seconds later they heard cries and turned to find Jacqueline ablaze, 'like a stunt man on TV', as John Foy insisted. The speed with which the horrific fire evolved obviously stunned them both. Both insisted that when they first passed by, there was no smoke and no smell of burning.

Both were instrumental in putting out the flames. Foy pointed out that Jacqueline seemed fine, despite having melted acrylic all over her back. She complained only of a burned finger, he said.

Karena Leazer and fellow hairdressing student Rachael Heckle had something else to add to the mystery. While passing the cookery students on the stairs, Karena said she saw a strange glowing light above Jacqueline's right shoulder. It seemed to appear in midair and fall down her back. Jacqueline allegedly then called out, 'It's gone down my back – get it out!' Thirty seconds later the two witnesses heard screams and looked back to see Jacqueline burning fiercely. Rachael confirmed this, although she thought originally Karena had spoken of a cigarette falling down the victim's back. Karena denied this and eventually both girls agreed it had just been a strange glowing light.

No evidence was presented by anyone that any of the three girls were smoking, or even that they smoked. But could a lighted cigarette have been dropped from above? Rachael Heckle now astounded everyone by insisting that the girl on the stairs *was not* Jacqueline Fitzsimon! Amazingly, she was not fully cross-examined about this extraordinary claim.

Three staff members, James Witton, student director, Alan

Harmer, lecturer, and Edward Davies, senior lecturer, then told how they had arrived on the scene after hearing screams and helped put out the fire. It had not been easy, and despite fairly nasty-looking burns, Jacqueline seemed remarkably free from pain.

Finally a key witness, cookery tutor Robert Carson, took the stand. He was adamant that the rings on the cookers had been turned off an hour before the end of the lesson. In any case, Jacqueline had not been leaning against the cooker. He stated that the girl and her friends had waited by the door to be dismissed at precisely 10.50 A.M. He admitted that, with a colleague, he had watched the girls waiting to leave, and said, 'I am sure that if she had been alight I would have noticed or smelt something. In over twenty years of catering I have never seen a catering jacket on fire.'

It was obvious that the jury should have a full knowledge of the special catering clothes worn by the student. To this end, Peter Hatton, Senior Administrator in charge of Health and Safety at the college, was called. Hatton claimed not to know whether or not the clothes were flammable. By now it seemed that the inquest was guiding the jury towards one conclusion – that Jacqueline had caught fire through leaning against a lighted cooker. This was despite all the problems associated with this shaky theory.

This line of thought took a further hammering when Detective Sergeant Geoffrey Abel of the Cheshire Police gave testimony. Abel's report was astonishing but, again, he was subjected to little or no examination.

Why were the police not informed until 30 January, two days after the incident? Why were the CID asked to investigate if it was deemed to be an accident? The officer, together with a colleague, visited the college, then interviewed Jacqueline in hospital. There she was sitting up in bed, 'looking positive, and in the circumstances, quite happy'. With reference to her subsequent death, the officer blurted

out, 'To be perfectly honest, what has subsequently transpired is amazing!'

Several times she had told them, 'It must have been the
cooker, I must have stood too near the cooker.' After leaving
C16 she had gone straight downstairs with Wendy and Paula.
There was no fooling around. They were not smoking. They
had been nowhere near the toilets. The girls had passed no
one smoking.

Jacqueline explained that she had felt nothing and smelt
nothing until halfway down the stairs, when her back started
to become hot. Within seconds there were flames, and she
put one hand on her head for fear of her hair lacquer catching
alight. With the other she tried to pull off the smock, but
clutches of burning material kept disintegrating in her hands.

The only solution she *could* come up with was that she
must have been leaning against the cooker, although she had
no memory of having done so. However, she admitted the
back ring had been left on.

DS Abel pointed out that she had already discussed the
affair extensively with several of her friends, and at the time
of the interview had probably already made up her mind what
had happened.

It is worth bearing in mind that if the college, fire service
or hospital had wanted to inform the police sooner, it could
hardly have been easier. The police station is only a hundred
yards from Halton College.

A service manager from the gas board, Leslie Mayo,
commented on the recurring cooker scenario. He stated that
gas flames could become invisible in strong sunlight, although
it was inconceivable that the heat required to cause smouldering would not also cause discomfort to anyone leaning near
a flame. The weather on 28 January did not indicate strong
sunlight – in fact it became unsettled with rain after lunch.

It now seemed we were leaving the realms of confusing
eyewitness reports and hearing from the scientific experts

who had conducted the serious government enquiry the public had been promised. This proved false optimism.

Philip Jones, a chartered chemist working for the Home Office, told of his visit to the college on 21 February where, along with a uniformed police officer, he conducted tests into the combustibility of the white smock. The ignition point, he discovered, was close to the hemline, near the bottom of the jacket.

An obtuse reference was made by the coroner to the possibility of a lighted cigarette causing the fire. Jones said that, contrary to popular belief, it is very difficult indeed for a cigarette to cause this type of fire. But he had held the jacket near the cooker flame and it had begun to smoulder. This smouldering had been kept going by stimulated airflow, which he speculated would have been present as an updraught on the stairwell.

Jones, under cross-examination, was asked how long he thought this smouldering would continue before Jacqueline would notice anything. Thirty seconds, he suggested, was the maximum before smell or heat would give the game away. Five minutes was far too long.

One of the solicitors then asked Jones how near to the flame the jacket had been held to cause smouldering. Millimetres away, he replied. Did the chartered chemist realize the distance between the gas jet and anyone leaning against the cooker was eight inches? And how many times during the tests had the smouldering jacket burst into flames?

'In none,' came the embarrassed reply, 'not even when airflow had been stimulated.' The best the jacket had ever done was smoulder a bit.

Next came a farcical interlude, although the majority of those packing the room were probably just bemused. Coroner Glasgow asked the Home Office scientist what he thought about 'Spontaneous Combustion'. Although the coroner misquoted the term, surely Jones realized he meant Spontaneous

Human Combustion? The man dutifully replied to the question put to him, and gave a curious lecture about how compost heaps and haystacks can burst into flames, adding that he had never known it to happen 'in these circumstances'.

Jones had begun with a theory that Jacqueline had caught alight from the cooker. Under cross-examination his certainty had crumbled, and he agreed that none of his evidence supported that conclusion which he then called merely 'a possible explanation'. He then admitted that 'my idea is by no means certain'. His final quote was that his hypothesis was no more than 'feasible'.

During the cross-examination which had demolished most of Philip Jones's certainty about his tests, a surprising admission occurred.

We were already puzzled as to why, at a fire death enquiry, not a single member of the Cheshire Fire Brigade was represented. The solicitor enquired if Mr Jones was aware that the Chief Fire Prevention Officer had carried out his own independent tests? Amazingly the scientist claimed to know nothing about this, and would not be drawn into comment. So the solicitor obliged.

The Cheshire Fire Brigade had requested an investigation by the Shirley Institute based in Manchester – a prestigious scientific establishment often called into serious cases.

Apparently this joint report was thirty pages long, and covered tests considerably more exhaustive than any Jones had carried out. When the garment burned it did not do so violently, and they could not get it alight from simply smouldering. However, when it did burn, flames were apparent within twenty-five seconds. All of this evidence, in their view, showed that the girl could not have been set aflame from the cooker.

Philip Jones would not comment, and we were left wondering why this very important document had not been presented as evidence at the inquest. Its existence had come to light almost by accident.

Peter Hough wrote to the Chief Fire Prevention Officer asking if we could have a copy of this document. There was no reply, but two months later his deputy, a Mr Sargeant, telephoned Peter at home. The conversation lasted three-quarters of an hour. When Peter asked about the report, the Deputy Chief Fire Prevention Officer replied that it *had* been sent to the coroner for use at the inquest. For some unknown reason it was returned as 'Coroner Glasgow had decided not to use the document as evidence.'

Back at the inquest, PC Jenion, a police officer acting for the coroner and who had accompanied the chartered chemist to the college, was called. We were astonished. This was the casually dressed man whom we had taken to be the court usher. He simply agreed with the Home Office conclusion and then, looking at us as he did so, stated that Jacqueline's family and friends had been very upset by all 'the nonsense talked about Spontaneous Human Combustion'.

'I have found no evidence of Spontaneous Human Combustion,' he assured the inquest, without explaining what that evidence might be, or how he would go about finding it. His tone throughout was quite arrogant. He was convinced that the latent smouldering theory was correct, but admitted that he had never seen a smouldering piece of cloth burst into flames. 'But it's common knowledge, isn't it?' he added.

Coroner Glasgow had opened proceedings by advising the jury that they must ignore all the talk in the media about SHC. Now, six and a half hours later, he concluded with a summary decidedly in favour of the Home Office conclusions. Through his brief summing up, he seemed to be advising the jury to conclude that the fire was a result of leaning against the gas cooker.

The jury could have returned an open verdict, which would mean the evidence was sufficiently dubious for them to be unable to reach a conclusion. That, to us, was the only fair option. Yet, after only twelve minutes, the jury, who during the course of the day had let a lot of ambiguous evidence pass by without resolution, returned with a verdict of 'misadventure' – an endorsement of the discredited cooker theory, and an outright shunning of SHC.

During the next few days, the media followed this party line with surprising tenacity. The local *Weekly News* did, however, refer to SHC, and to how 'Coroner Glasgow advised the jury to ignore the speculation that Jackie died from this strange and unusual phenomenon.' But the national *Daily Mail* of 29 June reported the verdict as if no controversy or contradiction among the witnesses had existed: 'Jackie, seventeen, had been leaning against a lighted cooker burner minutes before leaving the practical cookery exam,' it confidently informed its one million readers.

Malik Dhala at the *Widnes Weekly World*, who had carried our appeal for witnesses the month before, produced a major article, 'Inquest quashes fire death rumours'. He stated, with little regard for the facts: 'Rumours that cookery student Jacqueline Fitzsimon . . . died of Spontaneous Human Combustion were not true, it emerged from an inquest last week.'

We were aware that some of the reporters had not stayed the entire day, but surely Dhala, being from a local newspaper, had not been one of them?

Before the story was published, Peter Hough spoke to him and pointed out some of the inconsistencies with which the case abounded. Dhala agreed that the evidence for SHC and the latent smouldering theory were equally inconclusive, yet none of this appeared in the article. Controversy obviously was not the order of the day. The flames of the SHC rumour had been effectively smothered.

The verdict at the inquest reflected the need to accept a theory which seems dubious at best. How could the jacket have smouldered for so long without anyone smelling or seeing evidence of this? In August 1987, Peter Hough contacted Graham Littler, one of the cookery students. He was asked why he had changed a statement made to fire officers claiming Paula McGeever had told him she and Jacqueline had been in the toilets, and on coming out, she had smelt burning on herself. He remarked that he had been very confused at the time, and in reality was not sure who had said what or when. And although he had seen Jacqueline leaning against the cooker at some point, he was as mystified as everyone else by the lack of visual and olfactory evidence of burning.

Just how did the flames spread with such rapidity and ferocity? Why were such efforts apparently made to avoid asking pertinent questions, and to exclude vital scientific evidence? Why did the coroner go to such lengths to denigrate the SHC option?

Peter Hough spoke to engineering student John Foy, who had impressed us as one of the most objective witnesses. He had left after giving evidence, and we wanted to ask him what he thought of the latent smouldering theory.

'What a load of rubbish!' was his immediate answer. 'When we walked past there was nothing; seconds later her back was a mass of flame.'

But why was the important Shirley Institute report rebutted by the coroner? We are not attempting to propose that SHC *did* kill the student. In our view there are insufficient grounds to reach *any* firm conclusion. This view, and surprise at the bemused way the authorities had conducted themselves at the inquest, was shared by the Deputy Chief Fire Prevention Officer, as revealed in his long conversation with Peter Hough.

While not laying much store by the cooker verdict, Mr Sargeant is not a proponent of Spontaneous Human Combustion either. But did the authorities run away from the *possibility* of this answer, for reasons known only to themselves? The establishment automatically shies away from anything which contradicts the cosy order of things. And as American investigator Larry Arnold commented to Peter Hough, 'The psychology of "experts" confronted with the unknown has become as fascinating a topic as SHC itself.'

At the beginning of December 1985, we were both called several times from London by Bill Jones, a journalist on the BBC 2 *Newsnight* team. He explained that the news and documentary programme was planning a feature on SHC, and they wanted to include the Jacqueline Fitzsimon case. He was not very impressed when we would not play ball. We explained it was not *proven* that SHC was involved. Jones made it clear he wanted to speak to someone – anyone – connected with the case who would confirm that SHC was the culprit. We told him we knew of no one, and refused to give him a witness's telephone number until we had checked with him first.

We also explained that we were not prepared to become involved in a big media affair which would only bring more suffering to the Fitzsimon family. We suggested he contacted the girl's family direct. Perhaps they were as unhappy with the inquest verdict as we were, and would welcome a fresh investigation from such an influential source. His reply was, 'They're the last people I want to speak to.'

In investigating this case we find ourselves in something of a no-man's-land. On the one side are the authorities seemingly being rather selective, and on the other are certain self-styled experts on the phenomenon, who, quick as the eye can see, are eager to incorporate the Fitzsimon tragedy into the SHC mythos.

In the February 1987 edition of the American magazine *Fate*, a short item was published proclaiming that Jacqueline Fitzsimon's death was due to SHC. Since then, the latest offering from Janet and Colin Bord, *Modern Mysteries of Britain* (Grafton Books) devotes several pages to the case without mentioning most of the factors which detract from the SHC option. *The Hidden Power* (Chatto and Windus) by Brian Inglis, also reports the tragedy as a straight mystery. Just before Christmas 1987 came another in the series of Arthur C. Clarke books on the paranormal. Titled *Arthur C. Clarke's Chronicles Of The Strange and Mysterious* (Collins), it devoted space to the Fitzsimon fire death.

The men who actually wrote the book, television producers Simon Welfare and John Fairley, allowed the mystery to remain intact. Few of the doubts we had voiced were commented on. The reader, not having all the facts at his disposal, would assume from such accounts that here was a straight case of SHC. This deficient standard of reporting is just fodder to the debunkers. The truth becomes obscured by the confusion.

But an earlier case with SHC overtones *was* thoroughly investigated, this time in the USA, and the inducement was, not unexpectedly, 'millions of dollars'. Jack Angel, a well-salaried married man, met his appointment with the fire sometime around Tuesday 12 November 1974. After parking his motorhome (which doubled as a garment showroom) at the Ramada Inn, Savannah, Georgia, he donned pyjamas and retired. It was not until *four days later*, on 16 November, that Angel awoke.

His right hand was burned black on both sides from wrist to fingers. 'It was just burned, blistered,' he later stated to investigator Larry Arnold, 'and I had this big explosion in my chest. It left a hell of a hole. I was burned down here and on my groin, down on my ankle, and up and down my back. In spots!'

Angel's reaction to waking up and discovering this catalogue of injuries was bizarre. *Feeling no pain*, he climbed out of bed, showered and dressed. Staggering 'like I was drunk', he left the motorhome and entered the motel's cocktail lounge, where a waitress remarked on his condition.

'Yeah, looks like I got burned,' he understated, half conscious of his injuries but still insensitive to pain. Minutes later, the normally jovial salesman collapsed.

'The next thing I knew,' Angel told Arnold, 'I awoke in the hospital. And there's a doctor . . . with a pair of tweezers pulling skin off my arm.'

One doctor, he remembered, 'explained to me I wasn't burned externally, I was burned *internally*.'

Angel's wife examined the motorhome but found no evidence of the burning. Even the bed sheets were unmarked! In the meantime Angel transferred himself to a specialized burns centre. After examination, Dr David Fern said: 'This is a third-degree burn which damaged the skin severely and most of the underlying muscle of the hand, causing a total anaesthetic hand.' Also the 'ulnar nerve was completely destroyed' with 'the median nerve showing questionable viability'.

In other words Jack Angel's hand was so badly damaged it was as good as dead. Rather than face months of painful plastic surgery, he elected to have the hand and lower forearm amputated.

A firm of Georgian lawyers, hearing about the case, decided that the cause must have been an electrical equipment malfunction in the motorhome. They confidently told Angel that they would sue those responsible for 'three million dollars', if he agreed to hire them. No doubt the money would be more than useful, and thinking too that at last he might get to the bottom of the mystery, he gave them the go ahead.

Initially a thorough examination was made of all the wiring but nothing untoward was uncovered. Then weather records were scrutinized in case lightning had struck the motorhome. Another blank was drawn. In final desperation engineers completely dismantled and examined the vehicle. Not a single clue was found. The lawyers had to admit they were beaten.

Like Jacqueline Fitzsimon, Jack Angel initially felt no pain from his burns, and like the cookery student, he really could not explain what had happened.

Paranormal investigators Harry Price and Vincent Gaddis have noted that in the majority of mysterious fires the victims almost always cannot explain what caused the blaze.

Why then are we not prepared to herald the Fitzsimon tragedy as a bona fide example of Spontaneous Human Combustion? Because in this recent British case pertinent scientific evidence has been restricted, and the supposed investigation and inquest, in our opinion, was inadequate.

In truth, on the evidence which has been made public, there is no basis at all on which to state unequivocally what caused a pretty teenage girl to burst into flames, surrounded by fellow students. We believe it is the responsibility of the authorities, for the sake of the Fitzsimon family and any future victims of mysterious fire deaths, to resolve this case with the maximum efficiency. This has not happened, and we wonder why.

5

The Man Who Was Murdered By E.T.

Friday 6 June 1980 – a pleasant summer's day. The sun shone for a while, lifting the spirits of the inhabitants of West Yorkshire. The economic depression, though, continued to bite. This was a coal mining area, but the industry was now in slow decline, with many jobs disappearing in the name of progress.

One man without such worries was Zigmund Jan Adamski, born in August 1923, married to Leokadia ('Lottie') since 1951 and a miner all his working life. After suffering dreadfully at the hands of the Nazis during World War II he had fled with his wife to England and worked the coal faces of Lofthouse Colliery for almost thirty years.

The couple lived in a typical English semi-detached on the Tingley estate near Wakefield. They had become so much a part of the community that their Polish origins were lost in the distant past. People knew them by sight. Zigmund was a quiet man who liked a pint at the local, but rarely did anything more adventurous. His wife was confined to a wheelchair following a serious illness and this left him very concerned about her welfare.

With Zigmund's fifty-seventh birthday approaching and Lottie's health barely improving he put in a request for voluntary redundancy. Allowing his job to go to someone younger, who was currently an unemployment statistic, seemed like a good idea. The couple had no real money worries. The house was paid for. So it would be an ideal way of clearing the one big problem that Adamski faced: having to leave Lottie alone at night. Considering all the horror stories of rape and burglary this preyed heavily on his mind. If only the National Coal Board would agree.

Initial reactions had not been favourable. He could not 'retire early' and expect to get his pension rights. On the Wednesday he complained about this over a drink in the pub with a very good friend, Christopher Zielinski. 'Why won't they understand my position?' he asked. Nevertheless, the authorities had agreed to consider further and Zigmund could only await their verdict.

In the meantime, there were other things to be happy about. His cousin was on a two-month visit from Poland, and had brought her young son who suffered from polio. It was years since Zigmund had seen her and he was overjoyed at renewing their friendship. Even more exciting, the very next day Zigmund was to give away his goddaughter at her marriage. He had busied himself preparing a speech for the big day and was thrilled at the prospect of this grand occasion.

The morning of 6 June was spent in Leeds, where he took his cousin on a shopping trip. Bringing home a fish and chip dinner, to show off the delights of English cuisine, all four ate and talked into the early afternoon. Then Zigmund suddenly announced he was going out for a walk. 'I want to get some potatoes,' he explained simply to his wife and their visitors, before looking outside at the state of the weather.

It was 3.30 P.M. as Zigmund slipped on his checked jacket, took his wallet containing £20 or so and set off for the stroll of just 100 yards to the corner shop. He had a lung deformity, and suffered from bronchitis and this had caused a few problems with his heart. But he had never had a heart attack, he was not sick enough to give up work. Doctors had told him that if he behaved sensibly then there was nothing to worry about.

On the way to the shop he passed a neighbour cleaning his car. 'Hello, Zigmund – are you off to the pub already?' the man smiled.

'No,' Adamski shrugged. 'It's too early.'

As far as we know those are the last words anyone ever heard him speak. He did not arrive at the shop. By the time darkness fell that evening and he had still not returned home, Lottie reported the matter to the police. But it was the next day that doubts began to grow into fears. He failed to show up for the wedding he had anticipated so much. Zigmund Adamski was now a missing person. He had vanished off the face of the earth.

Five long days passed by, days of silent agony for the wife confined to a wheelchair, now in total despair about her missing husband. A small item in the local paper was the only report of her suffering. It did not note the irony of the letter from the colliery which had arrived, giving the hopelessly inappropriate news that Zigmund Adamski had been granted permission to take early retirement.

Other things went on which seemed to have no bearing on Zigmund's disappearance. For instance, late on the night of Tuesday 10 June a young couple in a house near the centre of Todmorden heard a strange commotion above their home. It was a fearful noise like 'great water surges'. Dashing outside they could see nothing, but as the noise faded into silence a beam of light poured from the heavens. A huge ellipse was sitting atop their roof, glowing green and red in dazzling hues. Silently it rose into the sky, bathing them in its bloody cast as it collapsed into a tiny dot.

Todmorden is twenty miles west of Tingley, a mill town on the slopes of the Pennines. It sits astride the Yorkshire/Lancashire border. What possible connection could it have with Adamski?

The Adamski family had no relatives or business there. So far as we know Zigmund had never been there. But this small town with its stone buildings cut from local millstone grit was to become the centre of the whole mystery, which to this day remains unsolved. For it was here that Zigmund Adamski finally returned.

Police constable Alan Godfrey was on foot patrol in the damp conditions of Wednesday 11 June. Adamski had now been missing for five whole days, but he had no reason to know that. Suddenly the police radio muttered some words that were muffled by his coat. '10–8,' he requested – a code which asked for a repeat of the message. 'Please attend the coal yard at Todmorden Railway Station ... We have a report from the ambulance station. There's a body!'

Officer Godfrey hurried straight over. Not much happens in Todmorden and this kind of event is thankfully rare. But he knew well enough that he should react swiftly. Naturally, he assumed that perhaps a passenger had collapsed getting off a train. Or someone had strayed on to the lines in a dangerous game of dare or ignorance.

As he neared the yard another PC, Malcolm Agley, joined him after also hearing the call. They walked through the drizzle into the small yard with its wooden bunkers containing piles of coal. The flashing blue light of the ambulance winked at them through the sullen air. A sombre-looking attendant came towards them and said, enigmatically, 'I think you've got a murder on your hands, Alan.'

This was a surprise. It is not the custom of ambulance staff to suggest the cause of death. But the scene before the two policemen was immediately suspicious. They could see the crumpled body in plain view atop a 15-foot-high pile of coal, greasy and slippery after the constant rain.

Alan Godfrey climbed the wooden slats that hemmed in the coal pile. This took him about twelve feet up and he could stoop down and inspect the body. The man was obviously dead and staring skyward in an odd fashion. His jaw was open and he looked as if he had died in some pain or distress. There were also small burns on his scalp and one behind the left ear. Carefully, the police officer moved the head and there on the back of the neck was a much bigger burn that was still oozing fluid.

The man's clothing was strange, too. He wore no shirt, the jacket buttons were in the wrong button holes and his shoes were half off his feet. As PC Agley laid cones around the bunker and radioed for the CID and a police surgeon, Alan Godfrey searched thoroughly for identification . . . a driver's licence, wallet, anything. There was nothing.

It was now 4.15 P.M. and the body had been discovered at just before 3.45 P.M. PC Godfrey scoured the immediate area for any clues, as the rain and the number of people in the yard might easily remove these by the time the CID arrived. One unidentified tyre track was found in the mud, but no footprints that matched those of the soles of the dead man's shoes were found in the black silt by the side of the bunker. It was very difficult to see how he had got on top of the coal pile – unless he had been placed there.

Trevor Parker, son of the coal yard owner, was in attendance and had found the body. He assured Alan that he had been at the same spot at around 10 A.M. that morning and the man was definitely not there then. The Phurnacite on which the body now lay *was* there. There were no deliveries scheduled for that part of the yard that day. With him was Peter Sutcliffe, an off-duty fireman, who stated that he had been in the yard that afternoon on business. He had last been near the bunker about 1.30 P.M. The body was not there then either.

Quite clearly, the dead man must have got on to the coal pile between 1.30 and 3.45 P.M.; although there was no sign of how he had done that. It seemed a safe bet that somebody working in the yard or on a passing train had seen something unusual that would help solve the riddle.

It was almost an hour before a CID Detective Inspector, a local doctor and Sergeant Tetlaw, from the coroner's office in Halifax, arrived. The CID were not very pleased with Alan

Godfrey's efforts to investigate the scene. They advised him, 'You are a uniformed officer – not Sherlock Holmes.' Of course, he was well aware of his limitations but felt that he had acted prudently under the circumstances and it was right that he should point out the evidence he had found. Even so, the suggestion that the dead man had fallen asleep under a truck, whilst leaking battery acid had dripped on to his head, was evidently regarded as more plausible than that he'd been murdered.

The body was taken away to Hebden Bridge mortuary, and matched up with missing person records. That evening it was finally identified as Zigmund Jan Adamski – who had vanished exactly five days earlier, almost to the minute. His whereabouts during that time, how he had got to Todmorden and how he had died were all mysteries of Agatha Christie proportions that were waiting to be resolved.

But, of course, the role of PC Alan Godfrey in this affair was over and done with. As he wound his way home that night, still smarting from his treatment at the hands of the CID, that seemed the only reasonable assumption to make.

In fact, the role of PC Godfrey was very far from over: it was just beginning. For soon the fantastic question was to be posed in certain quarters of the British media: was Zigmund Jan Adamski murdered by an extraterrestrial force?

INVESTIGATION

The post-mortem on Zigmund Adamski was conducted at Hebden Bridge at 9.15 P.M. that night. Consultant pathologist Dr Alan Edwards carried this out, with Sergeant Tetlaw in attendance.

Speaking into his tape recorder for the transcript, Dr Edwards said: 'The body is well washed and apparently well cared for.' From various factors he then established that the time of death was 'Eight to ten hours before my examination' – thus placing it at between 11.15 A.M. and 1.15 P.M. That, of course, is crucial, bearing in mind Peter Sutcliffe's story of seeing the coal tip at 1.30 P.M. without a body. The obvious interpretation is that the victim cannot have climbed on to the tip, because he was already dead. Somebody – or something – must have put him there.

Dr Edwards found only 'very slight' external injuries (basically superficial lacerations on his hands and knees). The burn marks were more prominent, but had been made before the cuts. Edwards said, 'The appearance of this lesion suggests a superficial burn or damage due to corrosives occurring a day or two before death [and] treated by application of an ointment.'

It was also noted that Adamski had not eaten for at least twelve hours before his death, but had swallowed nothing unusual and showed no indication of lack of proper food for a period as long as five days.

The lungs did show the effects of bronchitis and the heart was reasonably good, although there was a serious degree of constriction in the arteries. This was regarded as 'likely to be a contributory factor to the disability of the chronic lung disease'.

What was the cause of death? According to the pathologist it was heart failure precipitated by the bronchitis and heart disease and not in any way directly attributable to the relatively minor burns.

Assessing all the findings we have this scenario. Adamski was well cared for, wherever he had been. Whilst he may not have eaten or drunk anything during the last day of his life he had not been sleeping rough and he had shaved at some point on 10 June. His shirt, wallet and watch were missing, but there was no evidence that he had been assaulted or manhandled. Samples of the ointment were sent to forensic laboratories at Wetherby, but they were unidentifiable and remain puzzling. The burn had occurred at least a couple of days after Adamski had first gone missing, and whilst it may have induced shock which led to heart failure, this must have taken place at least twenty-four hours after the burning.

However, taking this suggested outline further, it seems that once Adamski had died somebody put the body on to the coal tip and left it – presumably expecting it to be found in such a prominent place. They presumably took extraordinary risks sneaking the body into the yard, somehow getting it on top of the coal without leaving any visible evidence, and then making their escape. It was broad daylight, remember, and the yard was in open view of the adjacent railway line and station.

They say that criminals make mistakes, but this method of disposing of a body (given the endless, bleak and desolate moorland totally surrounding Todmorden) seems ridiculous to the point of farce.

Unless, of course, this scenario is somehow mistaken.

Back at Todmorden police station the CID soon lost any obvious sign of interest and the case was given back to PCs Godfrey and Agley to compile a report for the inquest that inevitably follows such tragedies.

This was held on 3 July 1980 under the supervision of coroner James Turnbull. Much of the day was taken up with evidence from Trevor Parker about his discovery of the body, friends of Adamski attesting to the fact that the man was devoted to his wife, had no 'girlfriends' and would not just run away from home. Dr Edwards, the pathologist, repeated his views and answered questions, indicating that the heart attack could have been induced by stress, that the burn probably occurred on 9 June and that there was absolutely no evidence that the victim had been attacked, even in a minor way.

Mrs Adamski also spoke of her concern. She turned to the coroner and said, 'On his face there [was] something . . . he looked frightened.'

This very point had been noticed by Alan Godfrey, the

first police officer to inspect the body. But Godfrey was not at this inquest. Nor was Peter Sutcliffe, the vital witness who clarified that Adamski could not have got on to the tip by himself. PC Malcolm Agley was at this initial session but spoke only four sentences, in which he did not even mention that he was with another officer; although he did say, '[my] immediate reaction was one of crime.' Coroner Turnbull merely nodded, saying, 'Well, I have not ruled this out . . . I am not happy. We have not got a lot of answers . . . I am going to adjourn the proceedings. I cannot come to any conclusions on the evidence we have heard today . . . This is the sort of mystery which is intractable at the moment and we cannot leave any stone unturned . . . All I can do is assure you that whatever can be done will be done – I shall see that it is done, there is no question about that.'

Yet why were two crucial witnesses, PC Alan Godfrey and Peter Sutcliffe, not even invited to the inquest? It would be wrong to accuse the West Yorkshire police of not conducting a full enquiry. At the reopened inquest, on 4 September 1980, Detective Inspector J. Boyle of the Sowerby Bridge CID, reported on what appeared to be extensive investigations. Boyle said, 'In relation to the injury to Mr Adamski's head . . . enquiries were made at all the hospital out-patients departments, doctors' surgeries in the West Yorkshire, South Yorkshire, Greater Manchester and Lancashire county areas . . . I am unable to determine why or how he came to be found at Todmorden station coal yard. From enquiries I am satisfied that he had no enemies in the Todmorden area or indeed in any other part of West Yorkshire . . . I am quite happy that Mr Adamski died at the spot he was found as opposed to being taken there and dumped, but I cannot explain as to how and why he came to be found in the coal yard . . . None of my enquiries have helped me in trying to trace his movements on the Friday afternoon to the time he was found at the Todmorden railway station.'

This hearing was much shorter but did introduce a new factor: the story that there was some circumstantial evidence that might have led to kidnap charges. Detective Boyle explained that he had interviewed the man concerned, checked his movements and totally ruled him out of the investigation. Even so, Mrs Adamski was convinced that her husband had been taken to Todmorden against his will. She said so forthrightly.

Coroner Turnbull collected his thoughts and decided, 'I am not happy. Mr Boyle is not happy, but it may be that we will never know.' The suspected man was to be invited to answer questions at this final hearing.

Whilst all this was going on PC Alan Godfrey was becoming increasingly baffled. He had heard of PC Agley's visit to the first hearing, but knew that the inquest had been adjourned. He still expected to be called to present his evidence at some future point, and indeed assumed that Peter Sutcliffe's testimony was also crucial.

Godfrey had entered written reports into the inquest file, describing his own activities along with the testimony of the significant witness. So in that sense his duty was discharged. But he had become concerned by the manner in which every time he brought up the subject of the death he was told in no uncertain terms to drop it. Once he was even called into the CID office and advised that he should 'let sleeping dogs lie'. Yet at the same time the police were still reporting on their extensive efforts to find a solution to this mystery.

Suddenly, as October 1980 began, Alan Godfrey was to get a real shock. The local paper announced that the third hearing had been held on 25 September and the case finally laid to rest. An open verdict had been announced. Yet neither he nor Peter Sutcliffe had ever been called.

The final inquest hearing was solely concerned with a complete red herring, the idea that Jan Smolen – the father of the girl Adamski was to have given away – had somehow engineered Zigmund's disappearance before the wedding ceremony, because he was angry that his daughter had chosen an outsider instead of her own parent.

From the testimony of Mr Smolen, his estranged wife, the daughter and a friend of Jan Smolen's who was with him for some of the relevant five days, it was clear that these were utterly unfounded rumours, and Smolen was totally exonerated. He had no animosity towards Zigmund Adamski and indeed his daughter had first asked her father to give her away, but Smolen had declined for understandable personal reasons.

Now with no new leads at all, and despite several people commenting during the inquest that it seemed likely that Adamski had been 'abducted', Coroner Turnbull decided that he had no real option but to terminate proceedings. 'Frustrated as I am, frustrated as the police are . . . I cannot think of any other stone, at the moment, which I could turn.' But he promised that police enquiries would never completely cease, unless the mystery one day solved itself.

On the surface this seems like a fair and detailed examination of a strange, if sad, death. There is no obvious reason why the West Yorkshire police should even be suspected of a 'cover-up' and no hard evidence to the effect that they contemplated one.

On the other hand we have the considerable problem posed by Alan Godfrey's claims. One might dismiss the cautions issued against him to 'leave it to the CID' and 'stop stirring matters' as perfectly acceptable. After all, it really was not his job or his business as an ordinary uniformed officer. On the other hand, his actions appear quite sincere and reasonable given the circumstances, and he does claim to have been treated coolly.

However, much worse was to follow. PC Godfrey claims that when he made enquiries to discover why he and Peter Sutcliffe were ignored by the inquest it was found that all his statements had vanished from the records. This is an extraordinary claim to make, and of course Godfrey has no idea who might have tampered with the evidence or why. Several people, inside and outside the police, could have had the opportunity.

Godfrey says that during October 1980 he issued an internal memo to superior officers on official forms asking why he had not been called to the inquest. It was this that eventually led to the discovery of the missing statements, although Godfrey received no official reply and when he took the matter up verbally he was advised that it was wise not to pursue the complaint. The affair was over and done with and best left that way for all concerned, particularly for the widow, Mrs Adamski.

In the midst of all this debate something truly extraordinary happened to PC Godfrey. It was to elevate this case from a local 'who-done-it' to the status of a 'what-done-it'.

At just after 5 A.M. on the morning of 28 November 1980 the officer was in his panda car on night patrol. Some straying cattle had been reported bothering a housing estate on the edge of town, so he decided to have one last crack at finding them before his shift ended. He drove a few hundred yards northwest along Burnley Road, planning to turn right into Ferney Lee Road and swing back to the station if still unsuccessful. But then he caught sight of a peculiar light on the road ahead. Abandoning his plans to return to the station he continued straight along the deserted road.

It had been a dismal night and although it was not presently raining the road surface was slippery. Perhaps there had been an accident. But as he came closer he was shocked to find that a spinning-top-shaped object was hovering at lamp-post height above the road. A line of windows ringed its edge. His headlight beams bounced back off a metal surface. The bushes at the roadside were moving as if in response to 'wind' from the object. To all intents and purposes it was a UFO.

Both the car radio and his personal handset failed to function, being blocked by static. This is quite a confined area, though, and sometimes does create 'black spots'. So, propping the already prepared accident sketch pad on to the windscreen, he drew the strange 'craft'.

Then suddenly – inexplicably – he was no longer looking at the object. There were moments of panic until he realized that he was now a few hundred yards further along Burnley Road. He turned around, drove back to the spot where the craft had been and found the road surface here already drier than the road nearby. There was a swirl pattern as if a rotating heat source from above had evaporated some of the surface water away. He drove back towards the police station, but on the way encountered another officer who was on foot patrol. Godfrey told him what he'd seen and took him back to examine the swirl pattern. Godfrey asked the other man to keep quiet about the incident, and then returned to the station where he realized that one of his police boots was split, as if he had been dragged along the ground forcefully. Fifteen minutes of time later seemed accounted for after he had first seen the UFO.

In a daze Alan Godfrey wondered what to do. He had no evidence to support his fantastic story and if he filed a report then those officers who had questioned his judgement over the Adamski affair might well have a field day. After agonies of indecision he decided to say nothing.

But that evening, when he returned to work, he heard that three police officers from the Halifax unit had been on the moors chasing some stolen motorcycles. With each other as back-up witnesses they had bravely made an official report on the blue and white light which had passed overhead shortly before 5 A.M. It was heading in the direction of Todmorden, they had said . . . straight for the spot where PC Godfrey was patrolling.

This was all the encouragement Alan needed. He told his

tale, made his statement, and when it was given to the local *Hebden Bridge Times* weekly paper he was surprised, but answered all their questions.

This story, in their 5 December 1980 issue, began a long chain of media activity which became quite extraordinary. The initial story was simple enough. Headlined 'May the force be with you', a play on a line from the smash hit movie *Star Wars*, it concentrated on the Halifax officers' sighting and made several errors, including adding a fourth witness who had not been involved.

A small UFO society had been contacted for a quote, but seemed pretty uninterested. Indeed this whole drama might have ended there but for the fact that Mike Sacks, a businessman from Bacup – just five miles across the moors from Todmorden – saw the story and reported it to MUFORA (the Manchester UFO Research Association), a small team whose meetings he attended.

This is where we first entered the story, since we both belong to that group and were involved in frequent discussions and debates as the case unfolded. Primary investigation remained in the hands of Sacks and two other people who were then members of MUFORA (although all three left in 1984 when some of their policies diverged from the cautious and reserved line the other membership preferred to maintain).

The other two investigators on the case were Detective Superintendent Norman Collinson, a senior CID officer with the Greater Manchester force, and Harry Harris, a solicitor from Sale in Cheshire. Collinson conducted inteviews with the police officers involved and Harris video-recorded these sessions, for the benefit of the other half dozen members of the MUFORA team.

It was only after these interviews that Alan Godfrey mentioned his involvement in the Adamski death, as a complete aside in one of the sessions. In fact Mike Sacks had already brought the item to our notice, providing one of the local cuttings that had reported the tragedy. There were reasons why we had been vaguely interested, despite it having no obvious connection with UFOs. Of course, the peculiar circumstances of the man's death would intrigue anyone fascinated by a mystery. But more than that, our attention was grabbed by the man's name. Adamski is extremely uncommon in Britain, although, of course, found much more often in Poland. Yet another Adamski – George – had been the first person in the world to claim that he was taken on board a UFO by extraterrestrials.

It is fair to say that George Adamski's claims were often wild (including seeing trees and rivers on the moon) and few people, even in UFO circles, regard them very seriously. But he published several books before his death and even had an audience with the Pope, such was his phenomenal appeal. A cult still exists in his honour.

There was no relationship between George and Zigmund Adamski. But the name coincidence, which was at first just odd, now seemed amazing. After all, Alan Godfrey had reported his connection with the Adamski death enquiry and he had then experienced a close encounter shortly afterwards. Indeed, MUFORA had very good reason to suspect that the policeman's memory blank might well hide that most incredible type of UFO case – a close encounter of the *fourth* kind.

A 'CE 4' occurs when people see a UFO, lose chunks of time – five days has been reported in several instances – and, under medical supervision, 'remember' being spacenapped for a medical examination. The examiners say they come from another world. But this is not proven.

These extreme cases are also known as 'abductions'. They are very rare, but it was certainly possible to view the story of Zigmund Adamski's abduction as another likely case without too much liberal interpretation. Alan Godfrey's story definitely had all the classic hallmarks that were apparent to us as experienced researchers. That these two suspicious events should occur within half a mile of each other, less than six months apart, and be linked together by this quite bizarre chain of events, astonished and disconcerted us.

It must be said that at no time did Alan Godfrey suggest that there was a connection. Of course, he was not aware of many of the reasons why Ufologists found the Adamski death extraordinary. Nevertheless, MUFORA decided that it would be foolish to make public that a UFO group was looking into the two incidents side by side, because the media might jump to premature conclusions. Our enquiries continued in total silence.

In the spring of 1981 Harry Harris made an approach to Lottie Adamski. Now that we were aware of Alan Godfrey's remarkable allegations about disappearing evidence, we felt that the widow should be asked whether she was satisfied with the police enquiries. Nearly a year had passed which would have healed some of the emotional wounds caused by her loss, and she soon made clear that she remained desperate to know the truth. Harry Harris then freely offered his services as a lawyer. This allowed us to explore the case objectively and with integrity, and in the process it was possible that Mrs Adamski just might be assisted. And by doing it this way we would keep MUFORA out of the public eye and prevent misconceptions about *why* we were investigating.

Very great thought went into these decisions. We had no desire to be seen as opportunists preying on a poor woman's misery. Had we not been certain she wanted our help it would not have been offered. We also determined that as our one area of expertise was the investigation of UFO abduction, if no evidence to support this should surface we would not endeavour to enter territory that was beyond our scope. We accept any criticism that might be levelled at us. Our choice may have been incorrect. But it was a choice honestly made in what we considered the best interests of Mrs Adamski.

Several months of research by Harry Harris followed. At the same time he was attempting to act diplomatically on Alan Godfrey's behalf to resolve his own problems with the West Yorkshire police.

The police were not a great deal of help. On 19 May 1981 the Assistant Chief Constable, G. A. Oldfield, wrote to Harris in reply to a request that as Mrs Adamski's lawyer he be allowed to study the photographs of the body and scene of the death. Oldfield stated, that since the photographs requested were not required in connection with any civil or criminal proceedings he was unable to comply.

This withholding of evidence from the wife of the victim is perfectly legal, but might be construed as odd when the inquest had reached its verdict eight months before, particularly in view of other actions by the West Yorkshire force.

By this time several months had passed since the video-filmed interviews with Alan Godfrey. No memory of the missing time had returned to him. So Harry Harris and his colleagues made a private decision to undertake an experiment. This was to use hypnosis to allow Alan to relive the events on Burnley Road and see if he could remember the parts that remained hidden in his subconscious mind.

These sessions were set up with two well-qualified doctors who had practices at leading hospitals in the northwest and also treated private patients in plush central Manchester offices. It should be said that Norman Collinson was positively *not* involved in these investigations as a police officer, but in his role as a private citizen.

All bar the first session were video-recorded and neither doctor knew that Alan Godfrey claimed to have seen a UFO. This minimized the prospect that they would influence the outcome by asking leading questions. In fact, being approached by a lawyer, a senior CID police officer and a businessman (Mike Sacks), and asked to regress a police constable back to a certain date would very probably have led the doctors to suspect that it was in connection with some criminal act.

This experiment had a number of associated problems, but was conducted in a spirit of enquiry. Quite extensive information did emerge, with Alan 'recalling' a standard UFO abduction and medical examination by strange little beings. (For a detailed account, including transcripts, you are advised to read *The Pennine UFO Mystery* published by Grafton in 1983, which Jenny Randles wrote on behalf of Alan Godfrey and the three erstwhile MUFORA investigators.)

By the summer of 1981 it was clear that we were not going to progress any further with the Adamski death and there was nothing beyond innuendo and circumstantial evidence linking it with Alan Godfrey's subsequent experiences. We now saw these as a full-blown abduction, only the second or third investigated in Britain at that point. But the terrible death of Zigmund Adamski was as mysterious as ever. Mrs Adamski was informed and the case was effectively put on ice.

As the semi-official MUFORA scribe, Jenny Randles wrote a 1500-word summary of the affair for the UFO literature. It was standard practice to report key cases to fellow researchers, but it was decided to do this before the hypnosis sessions in the summer of 1981. This was necessary to take into account the lower credence one must place on evidence gathered during an altered state of consciousness. Alan Godfrey has never failed to recognize this, stating that he *knows* what he saw on the road – it was *real* – but his memory under hypnosis only *seems* real.

Jenny's article, 'A Policeman's Lot', changed Alan's surname as a safeguard, even though his real name had been given in the local press the previous winter. It chiefly told of his UFO sighting as he remembered it, reported that hypnosis was to be carried out, and mentioned the Adamski death as 'a preliminary teaser', stating that it was of 'no apparent relevance' and that MUFORA had abandoned work on what seemed to be just a coincidence. Very deliberately, the links were played down. Several of them were purposely omitted. Because Alan was still a serving police officer, no mention was made either of his difficulties with the force or the stance he claimed the CID had held. This was also specifically excluded from *The Pennine UFO Mystery* which Jenny later wrote.

The article was published in a magazine called *FSR – Flying Saucer Review* – unknown to all but UFO researchers. Only limited copies are distributed and it is not sold on newsstands and holds no interest for the media. The report was published purely as a means of informing the UFO community about an interesting and instructive story. Jenny Randles received no payment and MUFORA had firmly decided against going to the local or national press with the Adamski/Godfrey case. There were just too many complicating factors.

As it turned out, about a month after Jenny's article had reached *FSR* subscribers, several MUFORA members received odd calls from the *Sunday Mirror*. Jenny was on holiday deep in rural Wales, yet she was tracked down and forced to respond to phone calls and telegrams. Back in the northwest Harry Harris and other members were being contacted by reporter John Sheard, who insisted on knowing what we had been up to and on being put in touch with 'the policeman who was abducted'.

For several days there was panic in the group. Members suspected one another of breaking their trust or selling the story to the tabloid press. As a professional writer, Jenny was naturally a prime suspect. Her holiday was already in ruins, but she simply refused to discuss the case with the *Sunday Mirror*, despite inducements, as did several other members of MUFORA. This is why the prime investigators figured in none of the media stories, national or local, that flooded out about this case. In return John Sheard refused to give his 'sources' for the story, but seemed unaware of the *FSR* article, or the group's full role in the affair, since he referred to several things that were wildly at variance with the facts as MUFORA knew them.

On Sunday 27 September 1981 Sheard and Stewart Bonney told their story – and told it big. 'Amazing UFO Death Riddle' the headline screamed, on the front page. This was only the second occasion in British history that a UFO case had received that kind of media prominence. MUFORA was horrified. But how had the reporters got hold of the story?

The text itself gave us some clues. For a start, Coroner James Turnbull was quoted. Amazingly, he was reported as saying that he felt it likely there was a simple explanation, but: 'The failure of forensic scientists to identify the corrosive substance which caused Mr Adamski's burns could lend some weight to the UFO theory. As a coroner I cannot speculate, but I must admit that if I was walking over Ilkley moor tomorrow and a UFO came down I would not be surprised.'

A UFO investigator was then quoted. He was Graham Birdsall, now the outspoken leader of the Yorkshire UFO Society and editor of its magazine *Quest*.

Birdsall put himself across as some sort of spokesperson for the case, although MUFORA knew of no other UFO investigators who had at that time interviewed the key witnesses, secured access to the inquest data, or conducted months of tests with Alan Godfrey under medically super-vised conditions. To state, as Birdsall did, that 'there is world-wide interest in this case. It is the biggest UFO story for many years' was premature and catastrophic.

Another investigator, who ran a UFO club for

schoolchildren, was also quoted as saying that Adamski appeared to have been dropped on to the coal tip from above. This man, Walter Reid, was a member of the national UFO group BUFORA. His status as an official investigator was later revoked by the society, who were unhappy with his irresponible involvement with this story.

We later discovered that these Yorkshire UFO investigators had decided to look into the case when they read Jenny's article in *FSR*. Without bothering to talk to either her or MUFORA they had prematurely aided local press publicity, which in turn attracted the national reporters, and led to this incredible public exposure.

Fortunately, the *Sunday Mirror* did not get hold of Alan Godfrey and did not name him, thanks to Jenny's use of a pseudonym in her *FSR* article. However, the rush into print with poor research and based on quotes from people not familiar with a very complex case was evidenced by the serious errors Sheard and Bonney made. For instance, they claimed that Zigmund Adamski vanished the day he was actually found; that Alan had only recalled seeing a UFO whilst 'in a trance'; and that this had happened 'only hours before' the body was discovered – instead of five and a half months later. The rash conclusion that Adamski had been 'frightened to death' was also offered to readers.

During 1981 Alan Godfrey had become the village bobby for the small community of Walsden, not far from Todmorden, and was well liked. However, the local and national press explosion threw him into real hot water. The West Yorkshire police press office at Wakefield was bombarded with calls from journalists all over the world requesting interviews with the officer involved in the 'UFO murder'. He was quickly hauled up before the Inspector at Todmorden and asked to explain how the story had got into the press. Not surprisingly, he assumed, and was even later quoted in the local paper as saying, that it must be Jenny Randles' fault.

He desperately tried to placate his superiors by insisting that he had not talked to any journalists.

Meanwhile, Graham Birdsall had seized this opportunity to begin an investigation of the case. He soon learnt what MUFORA had learnt months before – that the connections between UFOs and the death of Zigmund Adamski were bizarre, but circumstantial. Desperately, he began to cover his tracks and back out of the story whose flickering embers he had helped to fan. On 4 December 1981, in a story entitled 'Local Bobby's Close Encounter Intrigues the World', he admitted it was just a coincidence, but quite incredibly attempted to turn Alan Godfrey against those who had worked with him, accusing MUFORA of breaking the rules and Jenny Randles specifically of unethical behaviour.

Whilst accepting that it may have been a mistake to mention the Adamski death at all, however carefully, in her *FSR* article, Jenny is quite happy to let the reader judge from the facts who behaved correctly and who acted irresponsibly.

The police were, not surprisingly, concerned that Alan Godfrey's UFO encounter was now tied with the Adamski death in the minds of millions. They had not sought this. MUFORA had certainly attempted to avoid it. Alan Godfrey had absolutely held back from suggesting a link.

But it was made now, and there was no going backwards. Even so, the most sensible course of action would have been to hope it all faded into obscurity, as the police were not allowing the prime witness, Alan Godfrey, to be interviewed.

Nobody could have predicted what happened next. With Alan on a week's leave in late November 1981, he was called at home by the divisional officer. Such a call comes very rarely to an ordinary copper. To be advised by this high-ranking person that he should give an interview to John Sheard at the *Sunday Mirror* – the very journalist who two months before had triggered the rumpus – left Alan speechless.

He reminded the man of his orders not to give interviews. The next day the officer called again and said that Alan *was* to give the interview. Indeed, he was to go to Todmorden police station in uniform, despite being off duty, pick up a panda car, and pose for pictures that the newspaper required.

Still shaking his head in disbelief Alan gave the interview, although he was asked to sign a minute sheet which sensibly insisted he only talk about his UFO encounter and not his involvement in the Adamski death.

Predictably, the story, which appeared on 29 November 1981, one year after the encounter, was another disaster. A front-page feature showed Alan sitting in his car 'at the scene of one of the most amazing UFO mysteries the world has known'. In half a dozen paragraphs the case was twice linked with 'the mysterious "UFO death"' of Zigmund Adamski, although clearly by the newspaper rather than by anything Alan Godfrey had said.

The main story, by Sheard, was on page 11 and was headed 'The Alien terror of PC Godfrey'. It too referred extensively to the Adamski death and speculated that he had 'been subjected to a similar examination by aliens – and was not strong enough to bear the terror'.

It is hard to imagine that the senior police officers involved did not anticipate that this was how the *Sunday Mirror* would treat this heaven-sent story. The day after it appeared Alan was informed that the Chief Constable was demanding to know who had authorized the interview. Of course, Alan had to name all those who had advised that he talk to the press. A few days later Alan was again hauled before his local inspector and positively *ordered* not to have any further dealings with MUFORA, Harry Harris or the doctors who had been working on the case. Whilst he was furious at this infringement of his rights as a private citizen, he had no option but to comply and cut the research on the case stone dead.

This incident was the beginning of a long campaign of attrition which seems to have been an attempt to stop Alan Godfrey becoming an embarrassment. He had been seriously injured several years before whilst fending off a criminal and had spent much time in hospital. Whilst he was passed completely fit for duty, as police surgeons had attested, the circumstances of the injury made it impossible for him to ride a bicycle. This had long been recognized. But suddenly Alan's panda car was needed elsewhere and he was ordered to use a bicycle. When he provided medical evidence that he could not do so, he was told that he would be charged with disobeying an order. So he offered to push the bicycle! The response was a transfer, miles across Yorkshire, to another town. This badly interfered with his domestic life. He had a seriously ill young child and his wife was pregnant again. None of this was considered relevant and he was given no option but to take the transfer, where he was put in charge of the cells and manoeuvred out of the public eye.

Meantime he had been sent to see the police surgeon in Bradford on the grounds that senior officers felt his 'UFO encounters' (he has never claimed more than one) might suggest a medical problem. Nothing was found. On 26 April 1982 he was directed to Dr Kay at the Stanley Royd Hospital in Wakefield. This psychiatrist conducted all sorts of tests to discover if Alan Godfrey were 'prone to hallucinations'. Again nothing incriminating was found.

After these attempts to quieten him, Alan was informed by one of the doctors that 'the officers who sent you here ought to come and see me themselves'.

By now Alan Godfrey was heartily sick of the way he had been treated since reporting his UFO encounter. Because he felt that a great deal stemmed from misunderstandings of what he had experienced, it was decided that the story should be published in a proper fashion. Jenny Randles agreed to include the encounter in one of her books, on behalf of Alan and the MUFORA investigators. But it was to form part of an overall look at UFOs in the region. This book, *The Pennine UFO Mystery*, was written in the spring and summer of 1982 and, because Alan was still in the police force, it had to leave a great deal out.

In the course of writing, Jenny recorded each relevant chapter on a cassette and posted these to Todmorden so Alan could check them over before the final draft was prepared. In some manner which can only be guessed at, another source became aware of this unusual method. Two officers whom Alan did not recognize arrived at his home one night, showed warrant cards and gave their names. They demanded to know what the book would contain and to hear the tapes which Alan had been sent. He refused and they left. When he later complained about this extraordinary visit, the West Yorkshire police denied any knowledge of it and stated that no officers of the names given worked for them.

Around this time, lawyer Harry Harris was involved in another matter connected with the book, but which Alan Godfrey was not a party to. Both Harris and Jenny Randles had been receiving strange postcards from a Soviet scientist at a research institute in Novosibirsk. After discussing the implications of this, Harry was visited by Special Branch police officers who asked to see the material. He was in this instance quite happy to provide it.

With the book written and awaiting publication yet another amazing event took place. Alan was told by friends in the force that he was banned from Todmorden police station. Such a step would be unprecedented, since he was a West Yorkshire policeman, based at another station in the division. Despite protests, his appeals against this went unanswered and he was reminded that police officers could only be barred if they were suspected of a criminal act, in which case there would be an internal enquiry and charges would follow, or else the ban would be lifted.

No enquiry or charges did result, but Harry Harris gathered written statements from several people, including police officers who knew of this astonishing 'debarring' allegedly given by a senior officer. That had been on 10 September 1982 and, according to their statements, the reason given had been that when Alan was at the station 'things went missing'. No evidence to support this very serious allegation was ever offered by the West Yorkshire police. Whether or not it is true we cannot say.

Another eighteen months of problems followed. Despite attempts to resolve the situation amicably, and hard work by Harry Harris acting as Alan Godfrey's lawyer, it became plain that he had crossed the system and that the only way out was for him to resign. On advice from the police surgeon, he decided in March 1984 that he should leave whilst he could do so 'with honour and a pension,' because sooner or later he would end up having to leave. The medical grounds under which he departed from the force resulted directly from the assault he had suffered in 1977. They were entirely physical. Alan, a brave and courageous man who had previously worked at maximum security prisons on the Isle of Wight and at Wandsworth, London, was at no time found by any doctor or psychiatrist to suffer from anything which might detract from his testimony.

But he was not even allowed to serve out his full notice period. His UFO sighting was briefly mentioned (without his knowledge) in a book by writer John Rimmer, published in the spring of 1984. The BBC saw this and asked if he would appear on a TV programme plugging the book. He agreed and that was the final straw. The West Yorkshire police advised Alan to hand in his uniform and, although he would be on the staff until June, 'retire' weeks ahead of the due date.

Alan Godfrey officially left the West Yorkshire police a very bitter man on 8 June 1984. He had suffered dreadfully because of the way this weird story had been handled. The blame must rest in many quarters. The MUFORA investigators must accept their share. Jenny wonders if it might have been different had she not mentioned the death of Zigmund Adamski in her *FSR* piece. Several other people must also question the effect of their role on this policeman's life.

As for the final word from the West Yorkshire police, this was delivered on 10 June 1984. By some irony this was the very eve of the fourth anniversary of a day Alan Godfrey must wish had never dawned. It was also the night of his retirement party.

Only one Todmorden officer joined the 130 friends, policemen and women who came to wish Alan well in his future career. Because some had to journey from other divisions of the West Yorkshire force, Alan applied for an extension of the pub's drinking hours until 1 A.M. on 11 June.

Such extensions are quite common. The Freemasons' Arms in Todmorden gets them without problem. But West Yorkshire police opposed this granting of an extension licence. With just days to go the local magistrates threw the police action out of court and Alan's party went ahead as planned.

The moment the extension time ran out an inspector and sergeant from Todmorden police station raided the private function and searched the premises for anyone drinking after hours. They later called this act 'a part of routine'.

Alan and a few friends were sitting talking and reminiscing about what might have been. Nobody was drinking, and the police went home, beaten finally by good old-fashioned honesty.

We can only guess what actually did happen to Polish miner Zigmund Jan Adamski (and it may well have a perfectly simple non-supernatural explanation). But we were not the ones who turned this affair into a circus act. Once that process had begun we surely had a duty to relate the truth.

We may well stand accused of dredging up a series of unrelated coincidences for sensationalist reasons. It may be said we have no regard for the suffering of Zigmund Adamski's friends and family. If so, we are sorry. But the case has become a myth, like it or not. And we perceive our responsibility to be that of recounting what really happened before it is lost to posterity. Too much ignorance has dominated this case.

Ignorance, for example, of what it means to undergo a strange and terrifying experience which you do not understand and did not ask for. Ignorance of just how brave (or foolish) it can be to talk about such events on a public platform. Knowing yourself that you are being honest is no guarantee that others will treat you honourably.

Alan Godfrey does not *know* what happened to him on Burnley Road in that early morning of November 1980. He does not *know* what exact fate befell Zigmund Jan Adamski. But he is puzzled by the way both these events were handled in public and official circles. And he did tell Jenny, in summation of this wretched episode, 'Adamski was murdered! I saw the body. No doubt about it, that man died a painful death.'

6

The Killing Fields

Snippy was just an animal, a lovable three-year-old Appaloosa saddle horse, somebody's pet. He was docile, easy going, a threat to no one. Snippy belonged to Mrs Berle Lewis, but was pastured at her brother's ranch close by, northeast of Alamosa in a remote area of Colorado's San Luis Valley.

In this mountainous region the land was dry and water was often scarce. Snippy used to wander for miles through the clusters of chico bush, but habitually came to the ranch house every evening for a drink and sometimes a dole of grain. He was a healthy horse, and on 7 September 1967, when he turned up for his usual drink, showed no signs of illness. But that was the last time he was seen alive. The following evening he failed to appear, and Ben King, Mrs Lewis's brother, was worried.

This was so unlike the animal that Ben was concerned for his safety. When dawn came and there was still no sign, he telephoned his sister and they went out to search. Snippy's body was discovered just half a mile from the ranch house near the edge of a clearing in the bush.

They stared in disbelief at the carcass. This was more than just the death of a beloved pet, here was something bizarre, sinister. The neck and head had been completely stripped of flesh, and the cut at the base of the neck was so clean it could only have been done with a surgeon's knife. On the ground was a black substance with the appearance of tar, but there was not a shred of skin, mane or hide anywhere. Even more curious, not a drop of blood stained the earth.

Mr Lewis arrived and, after consoling his wife, remarked on an odd odour around the horse. Berle called it 'incense-like', but her husband described it more as a 'medicinal' smell. The three then started looking round for additional clues to who might have committed the grisly crime.

There was an obvious lack of hoof- and footprints. In some places the chico bushes had been flattened to some ten inches high. A hundred yards away were discovered fifteen indentations in the ground resembling circular exhaust marks. In another area close to the animal, six identical holes two inches wide and four deep were found.

Ben King, an expert tracker, finally discovered some hoofprints. They belonged to Snippy and two other horses pastured with him. The three had been running in what was apparently a panicked headlong flight towards the ranch house. King said later the tracks clearly showed the 'dig in, push off' indentations of fast-running horses. Then the tracks separated, the two other horses continuing towards the ranch, and Snippy veering away for a short while before abruptly stopping. One hundred feet from where the tracks ended lay Snippy's mutilated body.

Mrs Lewis turned to her husband and sadly shook her head. She had loved that horse, and now it had died in macabre circumstances. Berle wondered if he had suffered before he died. The middle-aged lady shivered.

'I really believe,' she said, 'that a flying saucer had something to do with Snippy's death.'

America in the sixties was a hot-bed of UFO activity, but Mrs Lewis's hunch was bolstered by what her 87-year-old mother had to say. Agnes King lived in a cabin just a quarter of a mile from the site of the tragedy. She was found by investigators to be remarkably alert for her age. Mrs King reported that a large unknown object had passed low over her cabin on the evening Snippy did not show up for his regular drink.

Berle Lewis called up Sheriff Ben Phillips and told him the story. He declined even to come out to the remote ranch, remarking, glibly, 'Your horse was probably killed by lightning.'

But within twenty-four hours, first the Pueblo and then the Denver media prominently carried news of the incident. The tie-in with UFOs was further strengthened by several people claiming to have seen strange lights in the sky at the time of Snippy's disappearance. One of these was Superior Court Judge Charles Bennet, of Denver.

As the story hit the wire service, the police authorities in Alamosa received telephone calls from all parts of the USA, many callers claiming strange deaths involving their own pets and livestock.

Now the story was travelling around the world, but still no proper examination of the carcass had taken place. On 16 September Mrs Lewis, with some friends, returned to the area to hunt for more clues. She found something hanging in the middle of a flattened chico bush. It was a piece of flesh with horsehairs sticking to it. When she prodded it, the thing split open, spilling a green viscous matter on to her hand. It immediately turned red and started to burn. Washing it under water drove the discomfort away.

The growing media interest at last seemed to force some sort of investigation. On 23 September, Duane Martin of the Forestry Service came down with a geiger counter; he obtained some puzzling results. Around the carcass readings showed a normal background count, but some distance away radiation was way up. The exhaust-like markings too showed a high degree of radioactivity.

Mrs Lewis was even more certain now that Snippy had met a very unusual death. 'I discounted every other explanation after Snippy's carcass came up radioactive,' she said, with a degree of inaccuracy. 'For one thing, lightning doesn't do things like that. Sure as hell lightning don't boil all the meat off the bones and take it away and never leave a speck.

The horse may have been killed by someone conducting a secret laboratory experiment. Flying saucers are a more distinct possibility because we see something – I won't say what it is – almost every night. Almost any night you check the skies around here you see something besides airplanes, and it seems the sightings have become more frequent during the past six weeks. Lately, the objects have been like pulsating green and white beacon lights. They pulsate, stop, move on, stop again, then go completely out. Other objects appear to be just straight lights, moving fast across the sky.'

A month had now passed since the discovery of Snippy's body. Strangely, apart from where its hind quarters had been nibbled by coyotes, predators seemed to have kept their distance.

Next on the scene was a three-man team from the National Investigating Committee on Aerial Phenomena (NICAP). This included Herb Roth, co-ordinator of a United Airlines flight training programme, Kenneth Steinmetz, and Captain Dick Cable. Captain Cable belonged to the North American Air Defence Command.

They examined Snippy and the surrounding scrubland, taking photographs and samples of the tar-like substance, 'exhaust' marks, hair and flesh.

Not long after the NICAP representatives had left, a Denver pathologist arrived and asked to see the horse. For nearly an hour he performed an autopsy. Suddenly the mystery took on even larger proportions. Snippy's abdominal, brain and spinal cavities were completely empty. The pathologist, who requested anonymity, commented, 'The absence of organs in the abdominal cavity is absolutely unexplainable. And there should have been a good deal of fluid in the brain cavity, but it was empty.'

In no way, he declared, could lightning have been responsible for the horse's death, as the authorities were claiming. But Sheriff Ben Phillips was still adamant. 'The horse died a month ago, and we've had some warm weather, with maggots and other bugs on it as thick as can be. They're trying to make a big mystery out of it.'

A veterinary surgeon from the University of Colorado came out, checked over the carcass, then claimed he had solved the mystery.

Dr Robert Adams declared the horse had caught a bad leg infection, and after wandering around in a circle, collapsed. But the area of ground where Snippy had 'circled' was the place where Mrs Lewis made visitors stand, so as not to wander around destroying vital evidence.

In Dr Adams's scenario, a passing Samaritan had found the horse dying and decided to put the beast out of its misery by cutting its throat. Scavengers had then come and selectively removed all the tissue from the neck and head, including the mane and internal organs, whilst ignoring the rest of the body.

Jim Lorenzen, Director of the Aerial Phenomena Research Organization (APRO), spent a lot of his life around thoroughbred horses, on the ranch that his parents ran. He argued that Dr Adams's conclusions were grossly in error.

Lorenzen reasoned that even if the horse had suffered an infection – which the owners had always denied, that being the first thing they had looked for – Snippy would not have run around in a circle from pain or even agony. Snippy was a pet, not a working horse, with a close relationship with his owners. He would have rubbed the offending limb against a fence or building, and made it quite obvious to Mr King or Mrs Lewis that he was ill.

On the contrary, Ben King remarked that on the last evening Snippy turned up for water, he was playfully bucking and racing about. King would quickly have realized if anything was wrong.

But some of the sceptics went to quite extreme lengths to

devise an explanation for the death and condition of the horse.

Red Fenwick of the *Denver Post* postulated that someone had first of all shot Snippy with a tranquillizer pellet, then set up a block and tackle to dip Snippy's head and neck in a drum of acid. How all the equipment was transported in and out of the remote ranch without being seen or leaving evidence, even tyre marks, was never explained. A motive was not even considered. As one reader of the *Post* remarked, 'I'd prefer to take my chances with a Martian than with somebody who would do that!'

Just how did Snippy die, and why? Who or what made the precise cut around the neck, removed all hide and flesh, Snippy's brain and other internal organs – without leaving any evidence?

Snippy's death was never solved. The connection with UFOs (whatever they might be) was only circumstantial. As late as 1980, the Aerial Phenomena Research Organization were still driving home this point.

'APRO does not claim that Snippy was killed by "flying saucer people", rather that he died in a very strange manner and that his death has yet to be satisfactorily explained.'

Yet in the wake of Snippy's death was to follow a great tide of similarly killed and mutilated animals.

Lightning strikes or UFOs?

INVESTIGATION

Was there really anything 'supernatural' about Snippy's death, or was it all down to ignorance and imagination?

The seventies saw thousands of similar deaths hot on the heels of Snippy's premature demise. Most were equally as bemusing, with internal organs, eyes, tongue, lips and genitals removed with apparent expert surgical precision. Some of the work was so good that veterinarians at Oklahoma State

University stated they were unable to produce students capable of duplicating what the mutilators had done.

And then there was the blood. Or rather there wasn't any blood in most of the cases, either on the ground or in the body. That was the trouble.

The majority of reports came from the USA, Puerto Rico and Canada. But there were incidents in other countries such as Brazil, Spain and the Canary Islands. Mysterious animal deaths are not a new phenomenon, however. They go back a long way, albeit with less frequency.

Records are scarce and incomplete, but Charles Fort, a collector of curiosities at the beginning of this century, recorded these incidents. During May 1810 seven to eight sheep a night were being slaughtered in Ennerdale, Yorkshire. But all that was missing was the animals' blood, which seemed to have been sucked out through the jugular vein.

Then in a period of four months during 1874, sheep were preyed upon in a similar manner in Ireland. Up to thirty animals a night died, and in forty-two instances the killings were the same. Throats were cut and the blood 'sucked out', although the flesh remained untouched.

Most of these deaths were blamed on stray dogs; indeed, dogs were shot and in some instances the killings stopped.

The mysterious slaughter of sheep near Badminton in November 1905 prompted a Sergeant Carter of the Gloucestershire Police to say, 'I have seen two of the carcasses myself, and can say definitely that it is impossible for it to be the work of a dog. Dogs are not vampires, and do not suck the blood of a sheep, and leave the flesh untouched.'

Back now to the USA. Snippy the horse had come and gone but was not forgotten. The mutilations which followed spawned a myriad of newspaper headlines. 'Weird, Mysterious Killing Of Cattle Reported', 'Searchers Find Sixth Mutilated Cow In Adams County', 'Cattle Mutilations –

Ranchers Arming Themselves', 'Cattle Mutilation Number 84 Leaves Sheriff As Stumped As Ever', 'Cattle Killers May Fly Copters' ...

Bill Jackson, reporter for the *Sterling Advocate*, remembers the reactions of ranchers and law enforcement officers when they realized something awful was unfolding, something they were powerless to control. 'No one had ever come across anything like this before. Ninety to ninety-five per cent of mutilations were identical: part of the face was gone, an eye, tongue, ear and sometimes rectal and reproductive organs "bored" out of the animal. Usually there was no blood at all. Everyone was going crazy trying to dig up an explanation. There were a lot of strange lights seen and people talked about UFOs, satanic cults, dope smugglers and secret government experiments. But these deaths became so widespread people came down to just two possibilities: it had to be the government or it was UFOs.'

During the summer of 1975 over two hundred animal killings and mutilations were reported in Colorado. But other states were hit too: Wyoming, Utah, New Mexico, Idaho, Montana, Texas and Oklahoma.

The ranchers demanded action, and drawn into the debate were officials from organizations like the Mississippi Livestock Theft Bureau and the Colorado Bureau of Investigation as well as university pathologists and veterinary surgeons.

Dr William Fitzgerald is one of the few veterinary surgeons willing to speak out. In 1978 he received a request from the Sheriff's Office to carry out an autopsy on a six-month-old calf discovered mutilated in a remote forest in La Plata County. This was what he found. 'The anus and first four inches of rectum were gone, the first two to three inches of penis was removed, as was the left eye and one third of the tongue. A portion of the lips were "sawn" off. The indications are that some mutilations can be attributed to predators, but if this was a predator he has two feet and a six-inch knife! Removal of organs was made with very sharp single cuts.

Although I'm not the world's leading expert I work with knives frequently. I know what knives can do – I know the marks they leave.'

The calf was also devoid of blood. Dr Fitzgerald thought he might have the answer to that one. 'If a large-bore needle is placed in the jugular vein while the animal is sedated but still conscious, the heart will very nearly pump out all the blood. What is left will be kept to sequester blood to the liver, heart and periferal area, but the skin will be completely bloodless. Then you can cut that animal and there will be no bleeding at all.

'The animal was apparently restrained with something. What or why I don't know. It was washed clean – why, I don't know. And it was in a very remote area. Perhaps these things tie together. Perhaps whoever or whatever performed this didn't want to be observed. Someone went to a lot of trouble to get into a remote area where you wouldn't even know there were cattle to do this.'

Project Stigma, a civilian group founded by Tom Adams, discussed the case in the Autumn/Winter edition of their journal, *Stigmata*. 'No blood was found on the animal or in the area. No tracks or other signs were found during a sweep of a wide radius around the site. The area in which the carcass was found was reached only after a rugged rocky ride on a forest service road, and the area of the site was muddy. This was of interest because the vet found the animal looking as though it was ready for presentation at a show. The calf had been cleaned, combed, washed, scrubbed, the hooves polished, leaving no dirt or mud between the toes. Two small puncture wounds were reportedly found on the side of the neck near the jugular vein.'

Back in November 1974, Mike Rogers, Sheriff of Meeker County, received a call from a local farmer who said that one of his pigs had been killed during the night. This was the first recorded mutilation in Minnesota. During the following weeks dozens of cattle were found dead, classically mutilated. On one farm a mutilated cow had been discovered 'inside a circle with a perfect diameter'.

Rancher Frank Schiefelbein found one of his black Angus cows dead with its lips cut off, tongue cut out and jugular vein sliced. Even though the left ear was missing and the reproductive organs had been removed, there was very little blood on the ground, and there were no footprints, even though the field was covered with snow.

This looked like a typical mutilation mystery, and even though there had been a dearth of 'strange lights' – a common feature in other states – some individuals were quick to tie it in with UFOs.

The news director of Radio WYOO, in Eagar, Michael Douglas, took a personal interest in the case. He started sifting the facts very carefully, and something entirely different to UFOs started to emerge.

It seemed that someone, or a group even, was setting out to make the mutilations seem stranger than they really were. An autopsy carried out at the University of Minnesota revealed traces of a chemical which would cause the heart to pump very rapidly. The doctor who carried out the necropsy theorized that the chemical had been used to enable the heart to pump out all the blood, which was then collected in a container from the slit in the throat.

But how did the killers achieve all this without leaving footprints? According to Douglas, he found evidence that large sheets of cardboard had been used to distribute the mutilators' weight. Even so, one would have thought that marks would have been left in the snow. Douglas further claimed that a satanist group were responsible, using the animal parts in ritualistic ceremonies.

Investigators for APRO came to the same conclusion. In a bulletin published in 1975, they built the following scenario: 'The group would approach its intended victim at night, walking on large pieces of pasteboard. The victim was shot with a tranquillizer dart, immobilizing it (traces of nicotine sulphate were found in the livers of some of the animals). Then a heart stimulant was injected, an artery in the throat was punctured and the blood was caught in a plastic bag. Organs were then surgically removed with a minimum of bleeding.'

Both Michael Douglas and an investigator for the Centre for UFO Studies received threats from people claiming to be satanists. Although no arrests were made in Minnesota, over in Colorado members of a nomadic satanist cult were questioned.

Satanists provided a nice, cosy, relatively 'normal' answer to animal mutilations, which some people tried to use as a blanket explanation for *all* mysterious animal deaths. This obviously was not possible. It would mean a veritable army of satanists were at work day and night over many hundreds of square miles. And they did it without being seen, and without being caught.

Carl Whiteside, Deputy Director of the Colorado Bureau of Investigation (CBI), and no lover of mysteries, made this statement in 1979: 'The thing that has always bothered me in this investigation is the absence of any physical evidence. In my experience with cult type organizations, whether it be occult, organized narcotics trafficking, or anything which involves groups of people, sooner or later you will have someone who is a member of that group who will come forward and provide information. That hasn't happened.'

Some critics claimed all along there was no mutilation mystery, just animals dying from natural causes, with foxes, badgers, coyotes and magpies doing all the rest. No doubt this did account for some reports, but ranchers had been around animals all their lives and knew what predator damage looked like. Why should they and local law enforcement officers suddenly start going crazy?

Carl Whiteside, however, made no bones about it. 'Predators account for ninety-nine per cent of reported mutilations. Out of 203 reports we received, tissue samples were taken from forty-five. Of these only two were proven to have been mutilated with sharp instruments.'

Albert McChesney is a pathologist and co-ordinator of the Diagnostic Laboratory of Colorado State University. He talked about a 64-stone steer, with its tongue, ear, rectum and sex organs removed, to documentary film maker Linda Moulton Howe. 'I'm not trying to discredit the fact that there can be mutilations. But I just want to show that there is a good chance that something else could have caused it. That not all these lacerations and things like this are indeed from some sharp knife mutilation.'

One man who was not happy with the way the CBI were carrying out their analysis was Elbert County Sheriff George Yarnell. He was tired of being told that he and his ranchers were incapable of telling the difference between predator mutilation and that done with sharp precision instruments. 'Dang it,' he told the *Ranchland News* in September 1985, 'I was just pretty sure with my naked eye that some of them weren't predator-caused. But I'd just know what the results would be . . . "done by predators".'

Sheriff Yarnell decided to test the CBI, and cut off a piece of hide from a mutilated cow using a sharp knife, and sent it in for examination. Yarnell was furious when the report came back stating the cut had been done by predators. 'I had 'em fair and square on that one,' Yarnell said, and went up to see Carl Whiteside to confront him with it. Whiteside later admitted: 'I have no way to refute that. It was obviously an oversight in our lab.'

Sheriff Yarnell thinks differently. He sees it as an attempt to blame the mutilations on predators to 'save face' because the scientists are unable to solve the mystery.

Another Sheriff, Tex Graves, might agree. 'The cuts we

found were made with a sharp instrument which even we can't duplicate. We tried all sorts of knives, scalpels and razors on our own dead animals.'

Under-Sheriff Jerry Wolever from Stirling noted that in some instances natural predators had come along and mutilated the 'mutes', thus destroying vital evidence. But conversely, many ranchers have noted that predators have kept their distance from mutilated carcasses.

One rancher in Walsenberg, Colorado, came across a dead bull, as he told Linda Moulton Howe: 'We were passing down this road and there was a thunderstorm coming up behind. Even though we was rushin' we smelt the animal as we went by. Its sexual organs were all taken out, one of its eyes and the eyelashes were all gone. We didn't know what happened, unless it was a flying saucer or something! Being the pasture was locked up and had been for a year or two, and there's no tracks or no sign of anything around we could detect. Well, there wasn't no predators, there's no predators bothered it since it's been dead, even. It couldn't have been killed by a predator because all the surgical work was done by an expert. I really didn't think there was anything to it [mutilations] until it came home to me.'

If natural predation and weird cultists cannot account for the majority of mutilations, who or what else might be involved?

Ranchers and law enforcement officers were well aware of a number of unidentified helicopters overflying mutilation areas. In *The Cattle Report*, a short-lived news sheet edited by Ed Sanders, came a report of an incident which began around 10 P.M. on 21 August 1975, in Logan County.

When a helicopter appeared over the county which would not identify itself, Sheriff Graves went into action, and with two of his deputies, hired a private plane. Together with the help of seventeen ground units across the county, the chase commenced.

It should have been easy following the other aircraft; the night was ideal for flying, crystal clear with not a wisp of cloud in sight. But Graves and his team started to receive confusing radar reports allegedly from Warren Air Base, from people claiming to be airforce officers.

The chase ended at 4.30 A.M. in southwestern Nebraska. The lights from the helicopter were still clearly visible from below, when suddenly they went out. Tex Graves presumed the craft had landed, and ordered his pilot to lose height and overfly the area. They dropped to just over one hundred feet, but the only thing visible on the ground was a missile silo. Afterwards, Warren Air Base strenuously denied any knowledge of the bogus messages.

Just one month later, one of these unidentified helicopters was actually caught in the lens of a camera. The Sheriff's Office in Teller County, Colorado released copies showing a blue Hughes 500 helicopter hovering near trees with a man hanging or standing in the doorway. It was the Hughes which had set a world record for long-distance flying between Calver City, California, and Daytona, Florida, without refuelling. It also had the capacity to pick up a full-grown steer and carry it off – an important consideration when the indications were that the actual 'surgery' was carried out 'elsewhere'.

Helicopters, to a number of commentators, signified some sort of clandestine government involvement. But to what purpose?

At about the time the great wave of killings began, in 1973, a new branch of science – biogeochemistry – was beginning to develop, one researcher, David DeWitt, was quick to point out. Scientists claimed that by examining tissue samples from animals who had grazed on the same patch of ground for some time, the presence of various salts in their bodies could determine where oil and mineral deposits might be located.

Author George Andrews – a writer with extreme views on

the paranormal – sketched out a sinister scenario of Orwellian dimensions. In this, the CIA, acting on behalf of Big Business, might be going about secretly killing cattle and horses for these samples. Where positive results were found, ranchers, ignorant of the wealth right beneath their feet, could be bought out at a bargain price. The big corporations could then be moved in and the land plundered.

Surely this theory could easily be tested? Are there any ranchers who, after suffering mutilations, have sold out to 'outsiders'? Afterwards, was oil 'discovered' on that land?

Other theories included the United States government secretly testing for increased radiation levels after plutonium leaks, or testing the effects on livestock of accidental releases of germ warfare material.

Senator Harrison Schmitt, who said 'nothing was being done by the major law enforcement agencies who were trying to solve the problem' and organized a conference in Albuquerque to get federal government assistance, was asked by Linda Moulton Howe in 1979 whether he had asked the CIA if they were involved 'in doing some kind of environmental probe'. Schmitt admitted he had not, but reassured Howe that something as widespread as the mutilations could not stay secret for long. Having been closely involved with the intelligence community in the past, he was sure that one way or another the secret would have leaked out. This mirrored Carl Whiteside's comments regarding satanist groups.

Under-Sheriff Bill Waugh of Elbert County, Colorado, went out to Fort Carson in an attempt to shed light on the helicopter reports. He was told that for a short time there had been some intensive night training, but Waugh's opinion was that helicopters were not involved.

Another man who poured cold water on the helicopter theory was Lou Girodo of the District Attorney's Office. He accepted that helicopters were seen prior to or immediately after a mutilation, but said that none of the machines had been identified because they bore no markings. The reports also stated that the helicopters were 'silent'. 'And I've never heard of a silent helicopter,' Girodo added.

Now Sheriff of Las Animas County, Girodo has stated on camera that he believes the mutilators are 'creatures not of this planet'.

A hovering helicopter, creating a lot of noise and downdraught, would leave damage and send a herd of cattle stampeding. Is it reasonable too to assume that any government carrying out clandestine tests would not leave evidence lying around in the form of mutilated carcasses? If the animals had just 'disappeared', then the abductions would have been blamed on ordinary rustlers.

Is it any wonder then that some people speculated that the silent unmarked helicopters were really UFOs in disguise? Ufologist Richard Sigismond speculated that the carcasses had been left behind purposely to stimulate interest.

Also, strange lights have been spotted over pastureland, and while it has to be admitted that Jupiter and Venus never fail to fool some of the people some of the time, extreme accounts of UFO/animal contact have been around for years.

Twelve-year-old Everett Clark of Dante, Tennessee, had a lucky escape with his dog, Frisky, on 6 November 1957. After opening the door of his house to let the dog out, he noticed a strange object in a field opposite. Thinking he was dreaming, he went inside, but twenty minutes later, returned to let the dog back in.

The object was still there, and was surrounded by Frisky and several other neighbourhood dogs. The animals were being observed by two men and two women wearing peculiar clothing. One of the men made several attempts to capture Everett's pet and another dog, but gave up after a time. The four then walked through the walls of the oblong-shaped craft which promptly took off without a sound.

Another attempt at animal abduction allegedly occurred

elsewhere that same day. This time in Everettstown, New Jersey. John Trasco saw an egg-shaped object hovering near his barn when he went outside to feed his dog. As he drew closer, he was confronted by a three-foot-tall being 'with putty-coloured face and large frog-like eyes', who said in poor English, 'We are peaceful people, we only want your dog.'

Even though Trasco felt afraid he was not impressed and swore at the being, who disappeared into the craft which then took off. To a limited extent, Mrs Trasco was able to back up her husband's statement. She too saw the craft, but from her position in the house was unable to see the entity.

Modern reports involving UFOs and animals are almost non-existent in Britain. However, there was a strange incident in Frodsham, Cheshire, during January 1978. Early one evening, on the banks of the River Weaver, four poachers were out chasing pheasants. Suddenly one of them pointed to a silver balloon-like object on the surface of the water. As they watched, the thing lifted off the river and settled close by in a meadow.

Dumbstruck, the young men saw several figures in astronaut-type silver suits emerge, wearing headgear which included lights similar to miners' lamps. The figures then began taking undue interest in a herd of cattle grazing not far away.

By now the poachers were terrified. One of the cows was approached by the figures, and it seemed to become paralysed. A cage was then constructed around it, and some sort of measuring took place.

The men had seen enough. They turned and started to run, but were impeded by an invisible force which pulled painfully at their genitals. As they finally escaped, an eerie blue-green glow pervaded the area. One of the witnesses later developed marks on his leg, not unlike strong sunburn.

Linda Moulton Howe is a film maker and writer in

Colorado, where she was Director of Special Projects for a CBS affiliate from 1976 to 1983. Her work includes twenty documentaries and more than two hundred television productions, with subjects ranging over political issues, medicine, science and environmental pollution. She has received over thirty major awards. For her documentary on animal mutilations, *A Strange Harvest*, she was awarded a regional Emmy.

In May 1980 *A Strange Harvest* drew the largest audience for a locally-produced programme in the history of Denver television, and demand was so great that it was repeated just four months after its initial broadcast.

She has no doubt that a direct causal link exists between 'mutes' and UFOs. Her brother, a Vietnam veteran, told her of an incident at the military base at Great Falls, Montana, where he was stationed on helicopter duty. After a brightly glowing disc the size of a football field appeared over a missile silo, a SAT (Security Alert Team) was sent to investigate. 'The frightened SAT team radioed back that the disc was starting to rise. At about 1000 feet, NORAD picked up the moving UFO on radar and launched two F-106 jet interceptors. The UFO continued to rise. At around 200,000 feet, it disappeared from the radar scope. The story never made the newspapers. The commander of my brother's unit was also working with the Cascade County Sheriff's Office in Great Falls, which at the time was trying to cope with the growing number of cattle mutilations. One day the base's flight surgeon went out to look at a mutilated cow. He later told my brother that the incisions were very precise and professionally surgical in nature. He also said the cow had been thoroughly drained of blood.'

In her award-winning documentary, Linda Moulton Howe explores the Judy Doraty case, 'perhaps the first and only eyewitness account of a mutilation'.

Judy, her daughter Cindy, her mother and sister-in-law, were all driving back from Houston, Texas, after playing bingo. It was May 1973, and the night was clearly illuminated by the moon. Then a strange light hovered in the sky. At some point, Judy stopped the car and climbed out for a better look, but on the whole the family did not think too much of it, and continued on their journey. But afterwards, Judy began suffering terrible headaches and uncontrolled feelings of anxiety. Under the eye of the television camera, she was hypnotized and taken back to 'relive' the incident, by Professor Leo Sprinkle. From what subsequently transpired, one might assume that her conscious memory, and the memory of the others in the car, had undergone some sort of editing process.

Dr Sprinkle asked Judy under hypnosis to describe the light: 'It's like a spotlight shining down on the back of my car. And it's like it has substance to it. I can see an animal being taken up in this. I can see it squirming and trying to get free. And it's like it's being sucked up.'

Judy then feels she's in two places at the same time – still standing beside her car and also inside a strange craft. 'It's taken into some sort of chamber. And I get nauseated at watching how they excise parts. It's done very quickly, but the calf doesn't die immediately. There's tissue . . . it's laid out flat and smooth. It glistens. And there's needles in it, or what appear to be needles. It may be probes, I don't know. But it has a tube connected to it. And the same thing with what appears to be testicles. The same with the eye, and the tongue.'

Judy Doraty then describes 'two little men' with very large unblinking eyes. They convey to her that the work is necessary 'for our betterment'. Then Judy sees her daughter put on to the 'operating' table and starts to cry, tears streaming down her face. 'I'm just afraid they're going to do to her what they did to the animal. They put her to sleep, I guess. They're just examining her, but I'm so afraid they're going to cut her or something. They don't listen, they just ignore me . . . go about their work as if it's nothing. They don't seem to have any emotions. They don't seem to care. They just take some samples from her . . .'

In Dr Sprinkle's opinion, Judy Doraty is 'a sincere, honest and credible person'. However, hypnosis as a method of memory retrieval is highly contentious. Even though it has successfully been used as an aid to police investigations, no one is really sure whether a 'memory' of this sort is based in fact, or is just the result of some deep-seated belief. But the Doraty case does fit a pattern shown in many other cases where the witness, after seeing a bright light, seems to suffer a memory blackout. Under hypnosis they describe how they are examined on a table by non-human entities. In the American cases, the entities are nearly always small, with large heads and big dark eyes.

An unknown object was seen by many people on 5 July 1978 in Taos, New Mexico, hovering over a car. It left a powdery residue on the vehicle which was collected in a jar and sent to the Schoenfeld Laboratory for analysis. The material was found to be organic in nature, and had characteristics similar to teflon. But the spectrometer tests also found potassium, calcium, magnesium, iron and titanium.

A few years earlier, in 1976, State Patrol Officer Gabe Valdez and a man called Howard Burgess had discovered that the coats of some cattle fluoresced under ultraviolet light, as if they had been marked with something. When samples of hair were analysed, they were found to have on them a powder which was high in potassium and magnesium.

This seems to strengthen the UFO connection, but brings us no nearer to answering the question *why*? Judy Doraty was told by the 'aliens' that they were testing for pollution brought about by man. If UFOs are extraterrestrial spacecraft, and if they are connected with the mutilations, for what other reason might they be interested in fresh blood and anatomical parts?

The *APRO Bulletin* of December 1984 contained an article by Dr Michael Swords of Michigan University, who examined the possible ramifications of a recent discovery concerning similarities in the chromosome structure of cattle and humans. He asked 'whether this scientific breakthrough should allow ufologists to speculate that ufonauts are harvesting DNA and genetic material for genetic engineering purposes'. The similarities were so marked in some respects it had been suggested that, in emergencies, bovine blood could be used in human transfusions.

It was a Dr Womack who discovered that cattle chromosomes were far more closely related to human chromosomes than anyone had suspected. During a press conference, Womack stated: 'We must have more in common than was previously believed.'

But Dr Swords, who had studied the fine print, concluded that 'we have *some* identicalness, maybe even a lot, but we also have some non-identicalness'. In fact, according to Swords, chimpanzees and gorillas have more in common with us as far as chromosomes are concerned. What Dr Womack was excited about was the potential for cattle mutilations being connected to medical research, especially in the field of birth defects.

Dr Swords, in his paper, pours cold water on some of the more extreme theories put forward in the wake of Womack's discovery. He comments specifically on the alleged use of cattle DNA to build up human genes, and even whole creatures. 'Although this would make a great SF movie, it doesn't make much scientific sense.' He reasons that advanced extraterrestrials would be able to build their own 'human' genes using chemicals 'off the shelf', without needing to travel about the countryside leaving a trail of carnage.

'Okay, let's say they're not quite that advanced. They just want some "large chunk" of identical cattle and human genes and add them into a fertilized human embryo (say taken from abduction victims). This doesn't work either. Adding extra pieces of chromosomes to an embryo always causes severe birth defects, and the idea wouldn't explain the mass of mute cases (as this "research" would be limited by the available human eggs).'

This theory also ignores the fact that other animals with no chromosome correlation, such as horses, chickens, sheep and goats, have also been found mutilated.

American ufologists have a preoccupation with the UFOs-are-space-craft theory, and everything is seen in the light of this curious fifties SF movie scenario. Most British and European researchers, while claiming that the phenomenon does represent something 'alien' to mankind, prefer to keep a more open mind. And mutilations outside the USA do tend to display a much weirder pattern. Here the mutilation is often just the core of an anomaly with wider implications.

It has been argued that around 10,000 cases of mutilation have been reported in the United States since 1973. But a significant number also occurred on the island of Puerto Rico. The 300 catalogued there were more bizarre and 'Fortean'.

Engineer Sebastion Robiou Lamarche did a good job of interviewing witnesses, conducting lab analyses and sifting through a mountain of case material. What follows is a brief résumé of his work.

The first reported killing was sometime before 25 February 1975 in the town of Moca, situated in the northwest of the island. Next came a case in Aguadilla before the phenomenon spread with frightening rapidity across Puerto Rico.

On the morning of 18 March a farmer, Senor Hector Vega, arose early and found two dead goats with wounds from a sharp instrument under the thorax and upper part of the haunches. Yet worse was to come for this poor man. The next day, ten more goats had been killed and seven wounded, with a further ten missing altogether. The animals were not fenced in, making it extremely difficult for a would-be mutilator to round them up, kill and wound seventeen of them, and abduct ten more – all without making a noise, and without leaving any evidence.

Nearly all the injuries were around the thorax, most just an inch deep, although in some instances the instrument had penetrated the entire body. In all cases there was no sign of blood around the wounds.

On 5 April, at 12.30 A.M., Senor Buenaventura Bello fed his geese as usual before retiring. For some reason one of his dogs kept its distance, barking furiously. Later, around 8.30 A.M., Senor Bello came across ten geese and three pullets – dead, arranged in a circle. Each of the geese had a wound a quarter of an inch in diameter around which the feathers had been removed. One victim was later discovered in a neighbour's yard with the upper part of its body completely cut off 'as though with a very sharp instrument'.

How the killings could have been carried out is a mystery, considering Senor Bello's bedroom overlooks the yard, and his guard dogs remained undisturbed. Also, geese are ferocious birds.

The police conducted extensive enquiries, and the Federal Department of Agriculture found that the dogs refused to enter the yard.

El Vocera, the island's newspaper, demanded a full government enquiry. Dr Juan Rivero, a zoologist, scotched rumours that the mutilations were caused by vampire bats. Was a sadistic maniac loose, or could it be occultists? No one was ever caught.

Most of the victims were killed in the early hours. Nothing was ever heard except occasionally a loud screech and the flapping of wings. Wounds seemed to be caused by a punch, or sharp pricking instrument capable of cutting through organs and bone. What happened to the blood? None was ever found around the wounds.

Sebastion Lamarche noted that in five cases a strange very hairy animal was seen running from the scene of the crime. Don Cecilio Hernandez, who lost thirty-five chickens over several nights, claimed he saw, '. . . what looked like a woolly dog . . . with no legs or head . . . "running" off towards the hills silently. I never in my life have seen such a sight. It looked just like a mass of wool running along.'

Another witness told the press he had seen a 'whitish coloured gigantic condor, or vulture'. Maria Acevedo, who lives near Moca, told how in early March, at 12.30 A.M., she had heard 'a strange animal on the zinc roof of my house'. It walked about and seemed to be pecking, before flying off with a terrible screech.

Worse than this, Juan Muniz Feliciano was returning home from work at 10.00 P.M. when he was attacked 'by a terrible greyish creature with lots of feathers, a long thick neck, bigger than a goose'. During the attack, Juan called for his neighbours and drove the creature away by hurling stones. That same day, two women had seen 'a gigantic bird flying amongst the clouds'.

All of this is reminiscent of happenings in Britain around the turn of the century. At Binbrook Farm near the town of Market Rasen, Lincolnshire, *The South & North Lincs News*, of 18 January 1905, reported: 'Out of 250 fowls, Mr White [the owner] says he has only 24 left. They have all been killed in the same weird way. The skin around the neck, from the head to the breast, has been pulled off, and the windpipe drawn from its place and snapped. The fowl house has been watched night and day, and, whenever examined, four or five birds would be found dead.'

There were other things at Binbrook Farm, too, spontaneous fires breaking out everywhere, and an incident of a servant girl whose back burst alight.

Are all these things connected – are weird mutilations a form of poltergeist activity?

Sebastion Lamarche recorded a host of UFO sightings during the same period as the mutilations, including ground traces.

Willie Lopez, a disc jockey for Radio Rock situated on the top floor of the Darlington Building at Miramar, was disturbed during his show by three loud blows on the outside windows. Lopez saw a luminous figure making rapid movements, half hidden by one of the external columns of the building. Realizing he was alone in the studio, he telephoned a friend on another floor, but by 10.45 P.M. the friend had not arrived.

Going over to the window Lopez flung it wide open and was astonished to see a yellowish-white saucer-shaped object about forty feet in diameter, just a few feet from the building. He slammed shut the window, stopped the music, and told listeners what he had seen.

A publicity stunt, or had Lopez really had this experience? Lamarche claimed the disc jockey was in shock and on sedatives for several days.

The bizarre aspects of the mutilation phenomenon are further illustrated by these cases from Spain.

According to researcher Fernando Cerdia Guardia, the inhabitants of a farmhouse in Serrania de Ronda, Malaga, a popular tourist spot, were awakened by the barking of dogs one night in March 1978.

'We came out of the house,' the farmer explained, 'and saw something very strange. There was a human figure inside a metal suit. His legs were very long and cylindrical, like two tubes, and brightly lit by the light of the moon.'

Another member of the family continued, 'The "person", or whatever it was, came towards us. It was as if he was walking sideways, not forwards as we do. The dogs continued to bark furiously and we had to restrain them with great force.'

It was finally decided to set the dogs loose, but as soon as they were unleashed, the figure vanished. The following morning, over fifty 'foot'prints were discovered, between eight to ten centimetres deep. Then, close to the path where the entity had been seen, was discovered the mutilated body of the farmhouse cat.

A detailed analysis showed that the animal, which had been pregnant, had had its head and front leg cut off with an instrument which had also burned the fur and flesh. This was reminiscent of the damage a laser beam might inflict. The missing parts of the cat were never found, but the suited figure was seen elsewhere in the district.

Fernando Cerdia Guardia records several other incidents, including goats found with their throats cut, and two German Shepherd dogs who died within a week of one another, whilst guarding a factory. They were found with two symmetrical holes in each side of their bodies. Heart and liver had been removed, and they were drained of blood. No trace of blood was found on the ground.

By 1980, the mutilations had spread into Canada, where thirty were reported in nine months. Reports came from Brazil, also. Cases were, and still are, being reported in the USA, although their numbers are slight compared with the heyday of the seventies. One of the reasons could be that the ranchers just are not reporting these strange deaths any more. Many were openly hostile about their treatment by the authorities.

But even after studying the mass of data, there were still people who were saying it was all down to satanists and magpies.

Kenneth Rommel worked for the FBI for twenty-eight years, then in May 1979 he moved into the District Attorney's office in Santa Fe to determine if the mutilations were a law enforcement problem. He produced a 297-page report concluding that mutilations were made by predators after the death of an animal through natural causes. By innuendo, he accused the police of falsifying reports, and blamed hoaxers and the hysterical ranchers who feed the imagination of an uninformed public.

To those involved, this seemed a blatant attempt at a whitewash, with little regard for the facts.

In 1984 a book called *Mute Evidence*, written by Daniel Kagan and Ian Summers, was published. One reviewer wrote thus: 'This is a book that *had* to be written. Unfortunately, it should have been written by someone else. Bantam Books allegedly spent almost $100,000 on this amateurish mishmash. Dr Leo Sprinkle, Tom Adams and many others were, it is said, brutally and often pointlessly attacked in an astonishing display by two inexperienced and uninformed authors.'

When we asked Linda Moulton Howe for her opinion of *Mute Evidence*, she was just as forthright in her condemnation. 'The book, *Mute Evidence*, is not journalism or even reporting. It is a diatribe and character assassination ... it discredits those of us who tried, and still try, to honestly report about a subject the government wants kept secret from the public.'

On the subject of mutilations themselves, Linda told us: 'The most difficult area in mutilations is hard scientific analyses. It costs a lot of money to do necropsies and chemical analysis. Ranchers notify the local sheriff who sometimes makes a report, but often does not. There is no media coverage. The animal is buried or hauled off to a rendering plant. The way Tom Adams and I hear about mutilations these days is through a network of ranchers, law enforcement officers and other contacts who let us know what's happening. The mutilations do continue. But from the human point of view, it's a one-way route. Whatever is taken is not paid for. And what's left behind is fear, anger and dead animals.'

UFOs? Government? Dr Michael Swords issues a cautionary warning. 'We shouldn't dispense with the government testing theory lightly. If it *is* the government, and they are concerned about polluting our livestock and ourselves with nuclear energy technology, then we better not let them poison us with impunity by letting them hide behind an "extraterrestrial mystery" when the real mutilator is very dirty and down to earth indeed.'

Strange phenomena attract strange speculations, but the real answer could be even more extraordinary than those already put forward.

7

The Girl Who Disappeared

The village of Aylesbeare, Devon, is quiet and secluded. Nestling in rough heathland seven miles east of Exeter it has little to attract the tourists who flock to the West Country every summer. But it does have the sort of charm English villages can sometimes offer, and the campsites, holiday homes and occasional Royal Marine training exercises nearby do ensure that it is not quite as peaceful as it seems.

Things were to change on Saturday 19 August 1978, when Aylesbeare briefly became the centre of world attention – the focal point of a mystery that remains unsolved. For a few days, at least, there *was* something to bring notoriety to the village. This was all because of the unknown plight of one little girl.

Genette Tate was thirteen years old, a pupil at Exmouth Comprehensive school. She lived, apparently happily, at Barton Farm Cottage, with her father John (aged thirty-six and a sales representative). He had separated from the girl's mother, Sheila, nine years earlier, but they remained on reasonable terms even though he had custody and now lived with Genette's stepmother, Violet, and her daughter Tania.

Genette enjoyed writing poetry, was known to be a shy, modest and sensitive teenager, and had one main ambition, which was to be a nurse. This may have been fostered by her stepmother, who worked at the hospital in Exeter.

That Saturday was one of the best of the year. The temperature had risen into the low seventies and the sun shone from an almost unbroken blue sky. The lucky holiday-makers just beginning their summer break must have been delighted at their choice of week as they headed further south towards the more frequented tourist spots of Devon and Cornwall. But rain was to fall before the evening was out.

To the Tate family it was just an ordinary Saturday. Violet was on short-day duty at the hospital and John drove her to work, as he often did. He also took Tania and her best friend to the coach station in the city, because they were off for a short holiday in Cornwall together. The coach left at 3.10 P.M., and as John waved goodbye he was completely unaware of the drama unfolding back in Aylesbeare.

Genette had a newspaper round, like many youngsters of her age. It was an excellent way to add a couple of pounds to the week's pocket money and to obtain a sufficient degree of independence to buy things that she wanted. Although the route was not a long one, houses in the village were rather scattered and it was her practice to use her blue chopper bike to wend her way from house to house.

In fact, because he had the car out about the time Genette would be starting her deliveries, John had suggested that he take her in this. It would add only half an hour or so on to his trip, and it seemed a sensible plan. But Genette had arranged to meet her boyfriend on the round, so she declined. Through some mishap the boy apparently did not keep the rendezvous.

Because of such tiny decisions several lives were irrevocably altered. John Tate found himself forever regretting that he did not insist upon giving that lift. The young girl's friend may have blamed himself.

Genette wore white plimsolls, brown trousers that flared at the bottom, and a white cotton T-shirt with her Christian name embroidered on the left breast. She collected her papers from outside the pub and set off around 3.30 P.M. to deliver them to the waiting customers.

Within Lane is a narrow road that is pleasantly tree-lined and surrounded by plenty of fields, little thickets of trees and hidden gullies. It is a popular place to play or just to walk. As it was just a few hundred yards from Barton Farm Cottage,

Genette knew it well, and it was part of the journey she always made with her papers.

That afternoon, at some time approaching 4 P.M., she bumped into two of her friends, Margaret Heavey and Tracey Pratt. They were out walking and talking as Genette rode by on her bicycle. She pulled up and chatted to them for a few minutes, before waving goodbye and saying that she must get on with her deliveries.

Margaret and Tracey saw her ride on and turn a corner towards the village, then they forgot all about Genette and carried on with what they were doing. They idly walked along, a little while later turning the corner themselves. By now they had no thought of their friend. She would be long gone, taking newspapers to some other part of Aylesbeare. They were certainly not expecting to find a tragic puzzle.

But they *did* find one. Genette's blue chopper bike was spreadeagled across the lane and her newspapers lay discarded on the ground as if they had been dropped in a hurry.

'What has she seen?' was their first thought. Perhaps something had caught her eye in the fields or bushes by the roadside. But where was Genette now? There was not a trace.

Still only slightly concerned, the two girls called out Genette's name. There was no answer. They walked to the side of the road and called again into the trees. Still nothing. Doubts and worries were now beginning to grow. This was not normal. Something was wrong. Genette would just not go off on her own like this and leave her bike in the middle of the road. After a few more minutes of fruitless endeavour, Margaret and Tracey decided they could do little else but run for help.

Meanwhile, Violet had finished her stint at the hospital and John was now on his way home from Exeter with her in the passenger seat. They arrived back at Barton Farm Cottage shortly before Margaret and Tracey turned up, wheeling

Genette's bike. Bemusement turned into panic as they understood that something was truly awry. 'Where's Genette? What's happened?' John said quickly. Her two friends shook their heads. They did not know.

She was gone. She had vanished, leaving only her bike and the scattered newspapers as a clue to her distress.

John went immediately to see Constable Laws, the village bobby. He went to the site and checked out the situation for himself. By now, mildly annoyed customers were calling to enquire about the whereabouts of their papers. They were told about the mystery.

Within a couple of hours the position was clear. Genette Tate really was missing. Darkness would be falling soon, and the first hint of rain was on its way. Villagers got together to scour the heath, calling her name loudly and desperately.

There was no sign of the girl. Not a trace. She had gone so rapidly and unexpectedly. Hopes lingered that perhaps she had set off for some unplanned visit to a friend's house or another village. But why leave her bike and abandon the newspapers? That was just not like Genette. Not like her at all.

Those who knew the youngster already sensed that something was terribly wrong. But a full-scale police search would have to wait until the morning.

Before long all of East Devon would know of Genette's disappearance, and it was becoming very apparent that this was not just a girl taking off on some innocent jaunt. It was much worse than that.

She had vanished. Genette Tate had turned the corner and encountered her unknown fate. As each hour passed, fears for her safety would rise. Hopes for her return would fade.

But what had happened to that bright and happy young girl? Nobody had the first idea. It was a complete and total mystery. Exactly the sort of case, high on human drama and lacking in hard evidence, to bring amateur detectives scuttling out of the woodwork.

These detectives were of the conventional and the unconventional kinds. From would-be Sherlock Holmeses and Miss Marpleses, truly wanting to help solve the riddle, to psychics of one sort or another. As the news spread, they began to make their way towards Aylesbeare, determined to help in any way they could.

But was their help to prove an advantage or a hindrance?

INVESTIGATION

Sunday 20 August 1978 saw Aylesbeare buzzing with police and local people trying hard to find some trace of Genette. It is not usual to treat a person as missing so quickly, but the circumstances of this case were such that it was immediately obvious to the authorities that foul play might well be at work.

Children, unfortunately, do get kidnapped, attacked, even raped or murdered. Those thoughts crossed everybody's mind right from the start. But first a massive search had to be launched, examining every possible ditch or pond where she might accidentally have stumbled or collapsed. Perhaps she was lying injured somewhere, crying for help.

Yet the day ended without a single clue being found. There was no sign of a disturbance. If Genette had been attacked, where had the attacker come from? Where had he taken her afterwards? The area around Within Lane was checked and rechecked. Every inch was probed in minute detail. Nothing whatsoever was found. Yet Margaret Heavey and Tracey Pratt had been standing just around the corner from where this surmised attack took place. If the attacker had used a vehicle, why had they not seen or heard one? Why had Genette not screamed?

It was all very puzzling indeed.

The rest of the world learnt of the case on Monday 21 August. Most of the British national papers carried reasonably full accounts and TV news broadcasts reported the mystery. For a few days it was a topical story, but topicality fades very quickly in cases of this sort. Well before a week had passed, because there were no new leads and nothing else to write about, the tragedy had gradually worked itself further and further away from the front pages and its column inches decreased until it became invisible. The police knew that, even in Devon, it would be treated as 'old news' before much longer and they were desperate for some new leads.

Help was drafted in from as far away as Avon and Somerset to continue the search in ever more detail. With such disappearances, where it is considered highly improbable that the victim has simply run off, but a criminal act is strongly suspected, there is almost always some hint of what took place. The intensive searches that are mounted usually turn up the body, at least there is something belonging to the vanished person found nearby, such as an item of clothing. Alternatively there might be witnesses who saw or heard something important, or noticed strangers in the village.

In this case there were no such clues. Genette had literally turned the corner, dropped her bicycle, scattered her newspapers and vanished off the face of the earth. It was hardly surprising that by Wednesday the 23rd the Chief Constable of Devon and Cornwall, John Alderson, was quoted as saying, 'At the moment it is rather like the *Marie Celeste* mystery . . . we are using every conventional method of inquiry and even some unconventional ones . . . There is a temptation to clutch at straws.'

A number of plans were initiated to prise out the information that did not come naturally. John Tate was allowed to stage a press conference at which he made an emotive appeal to his missing daughter: 'If you are able to do anything off your own bat, then please telephone us, go to a policeman or even write.' To the public he pleaded, 'Please keep looking.

Do not give up hope.' But he was forced to admit, 'I fear she may have been abducted.'

On Tuesday the 22nd the police arranged a reconstruction of the disappearance, using a close friend of Genette's who was of a similar height and build but who did not want to be named. She wore identical clothes, and in front of whirring cameras and hovering reporters went through the final minutes of Genette's newspaper round. The hope was that this would jog somebody's memory about something they had seen on the Saturday. It was also a good way to get the story a big spot on the TV news broadcasts.

This desperate ploy paid off – or at least so it seemed. A couple half a mile from where the chopper bike was found recalled seeing a silver Mini with a young man at the wheel racing through the village at high speed. This was around the correct time. The police excitedly described it as 'the most valuable clue so far', but within twenty-four hours the car driver voluntarily came forward and had been positively eliminated from the investigation.

On Friday the 25th, The *Guardian* summed up the case in one of its final reports, saying, 'Police are facing one of the most puzzling disappearances on record. No evidence has been found. No fact uncovered to suggest what might have happened to Genette.'

One week after the disappearance came another move to assist the flagging enquiries. Police chief Alderson appealed to holidaymakers in the area to give up a few hours to come to Aylesbeare and help with the search. It turned out to be the biggest such operation ever mounted; 7000 citizens joined the hundreds of police and CID drafted in to scour the entire area. Once again nothing was found.

Of course, there were the inevitable jokers in the pack. One man was arrested in Chester after making a hoax ransom call to the Tates, an action the police described as 'despicable'. Even the local vicar, who set up an all-night vigil by a hotline phone urging anyone who might know something to 'confess' in confidence, only received dozens of hoax calls for his pains. And there was a brief flap of excitement when a note, apparently written by a young girl, was found on a road near Machynlleth, mid-Wales. It claimed to be from the victim of a kidnap and pleaded for help. Police were on the verge of moving the enquiry *en masse* up north when a 15-year-old girl came forward and admitted she had written the note as a game, when riding in her family car. It had accidentally blown out of the window. Police thanked her for having the courage to be honest and save vast amounts of time and money from being wasted.

Meanwhile, in a show of generosity, the *Exeter Express and Echo*, the evening newspaper which Genette had been delivering when she disappeared, offered a £1000 reward for anyone who could help to solve the mystery. Ten years later that money remained unclaimed.

Given all these failures, it is hardly surprising that, to use Chief Constable John Alderson's words, 'unconventional methods' were adopted. These mainly seem to have been to accept, if not exactly seek out, offers of assistance from amateur and professional mediums or psychics.

Roger Busby, senior public relations officer with the Devon and Cornwall police at the time, is still with the force. He remembers the matter well and fielded many of the calls from these people, who believed that their 'supernatural powers' might to able to assist in finding the missing girl.

He told us: 'This was a peculiar, almost unique set of circumstances . . . it lent itself to psychic involvement. But it was a one-off. Normally we wouldn't want this kind of help.'

John Alderson, now retired, was the Chief Constable whose public statements led to a flood of offers from mediums. He kindly granted us an interview on this matter and answered certain charges that had been levelled, suggesting he had a bit of an obsession with occult methods of policing. 'We decided as part of our strategy to detect that the case needed a high profile ... This in turn attracted people like mediums to offer their services. As a police force we have no expertise in these matters – and had no clues on the case – so you do tend to grasp at straws. After all, it may be that someone might have some special skill or instinct, rather like water diviners have. So we didn't say no. But we positively did not treat it on the same level as we would treat hard information.'

These words will no doubt reassure John Tate, father of the missing girl. For he has been one of the biggest critics of Chief Constable Alderson's decision to allow the psychics any involvement. He has said on this matter, 'I now strongly question whether the police were right to adopt such an attitude. An awful lot of psychics became involved in Genette's case ... But was it right to devote precious police time and money to this? Did it mean that a "psychic vision" was being "investigated" while real, solid, large as life avenues were neglected or ignored completely?'

He feels that the psychics 'rode roughshod over our feelings – which were in a desperate state already ... The influence of psychics started to have an unpleasant effect. Even when we didn't want them they were there, on our doorstep, always expecting to be met with an open door.'

Melvyn Harris, author of a book with the uncompromising title *Sorry, You've Been Duped* (Weidenfeld and Nicolson, 1986), is a man who tries to debunk all things paranormal. It is hardly astonishing that he champions John Tate's cause. Citing Tate's personal account of the aftermath to this tragedy (*Genette: Where Is She Now?*, Lion Books, 1985), he reports how Frances Dymond from Perranporth became involved in the case.

Ms Dymond is a well-known West Country medium, with whom we have come into contact on a number of occasions.

She claims to have had all manner of bizarre experiences and contacts with 'alien' figures. Harris claims that her 'spirit guides' had informed her that Genette had been strangled, taken to Exeter and buried in the walls of a house with bay windows, where presumably she remains to this day. The problem is that such a description could fit half the buildings in that city!

Melvyn Harris says that she refused to co-operate further with the police because her guides told her not to. However, as we understand from her, the police could simply gain nothing from her because of the vagueness of psychic visions. They do not 'turn on and off like a tap' she feels it necessary to explain.

Melvyn Harris further quotes from John Tate's book: 'The promises of the psychics were all lies. They raised false hopes in us.'

However, Harris was clearly influenced by his personal lack of conviction about such matters. For instance, he says Roger Busby felt psychics were only out to promote themselves and did not assist. Busby denied that to us. Harris also cites two entirely different sets of figures for the number of approaches received from psychics by the Devon police. One of these was 1200, which seems astonishingly high. Roger Busby could not give precise figures, but felt that this was an exaggeration.

We also have to question the total objectivity of John Tate himself. For his life went through dramatic changes after the disappearance of his daughter. He had major emotional problems in his past, primarily relationship with his step-daughter which, he bravely talked about. This provoked suggestions that he might be capable of harming his own daughter. Police enquiries into this scandal received a lot of media attention. John Tate admitted his misdeeds and the public disclosure of these matters brought enormous new pressure to bear on the Tate family. Sensibly, the police decided they had all suffered enough, took no action and also found absolutely nothing to link John Tate with Genette's disappearance.

Later Tate had an affair with a radio operator at a taxi company, and his second wife, Violet, sued for divorce. John gave their story to a national newspaper, who secreted the eloping couple away. They wished to protect their exclusive before revealing the matter with a front-page headline. In this, John's girlfriend, Kathy, was evocatively described as a 'scarlet woman' in the style beloved of the Sunday tabloids, and violent quarrels erupted over this publicity.

According to John Tate, Kathy from this point onwards became 'possessed of evil' and her rages were the product of devils. In an attempt to cure her he contacted a Christian fellowship in Exeter, and the group worked hard to drive out the 'demon' which they were able to convince both John and Kathy had now taken control of their lives.

John Tate describes a scene like something out of the movie *The Exorcist*: the demon-possessed Kathy was about to throw scalding coffee at him when he cried out to the Lord and she crumpled into a heap on the floor. The fellowship subsequently told them that they had been praying at the precise moment of this 'exorcism', and John acknowledged how he and his girlfriend 'felt that something had happened'.

Various other feelings, impulses and messages are related by John Tate in his book, such as the time they both 'knew' they had to go to Exeter. Here they found a man waiting to convert them both to active Christianity. The fellowship explained how the paranormal was full of evil and how Kathy 'needed to be freed from the grip the mediums and psychics had over her'. The theory was that the psychics who had tried to find Genette, and who had at first held a curious fascination for them both, were now somehow controlling Kathy's mind.

Then John began to have 'vivid hallucinations' of a beautiful land full of colour, where voices encouraged him to act more positively and not try to kill himself, as he had recently attempted.

We recount these details simply because it seems that John Tate was having exactly the same sort of 'visions' and 'feelings' as those described by the psychics whom he was readily denouncing. He now said, 'Satan, the devil, or whatever you like to call him, is very anxious to stop us doing a good job. He is the one who is behind the work of all the psychics and mediums, whether they realize it or not.'

Just one example will reveal his contradictory attitude. It took place on 25 August 1978, less than a week after Genette had disappeared and more than two years before John Tate became converted to this satanistic view of psychics.

On this Friday a medium came to call and took Violet away for a private chat. John was utterly exhausted by the seemingly endless searches of the past few days. So he went to lie down on the bed. He says he was in that limbo state one sometimes enters between sleep and wakefulness, when psychics, incidentally, often claim their visions come to them. He saw 'very clearly in my mind a blue MGB sports car with a black drophead. Then the scene changed and I was looking at a ruined castle tower with ivy climbing up the walls. Part of the wall had crumbled away and I could see the large blocks of scattered stone.' He still has no idea where this place is, but feels it might be connected with his daughter's disappearance.

Now, whether this vision was pure imagination brought on by tiredness, simple wish fulfilment or something more, it is precisely the sort of thing that psychics were reporting to the police. John Tate reported this one. Was he under the influence of Satan when doing so? Or was he merely offering information which might possibly help in some way? It shows how readily your beliefs can colour your interpretation of events.

It is interesting to compare the version of events given to us by the psychic who was present on that Friday and who supposedly triggered this vision in John Tate. The two display some significant differences.

The psychic was Bob Cracknell, a thickset, bearded man with a colourful past who toured the country living as a down and out before settling into an ordinary family life. Jenny has observed him demonstrate his alleged psychic abilities in his native town of Leicester and was reasonably impressed by his success at controlled experiments.

The experiments were set up by Kevin McClure, former editor of the paranormal research journal *Common Ground*, which was admirably open-minded but sceptical. McClure is quite a good friend of Colin Wilson, the acclaimed writer on murder, crime and the occult. Upon Kevin McClure's advice, Wilson had decided to supply the introduction to Bob Cracknell's fascinating life story (*Clues to the Unknown*, Hamlyn, 1981). This brought about a friendship between the author and the psychic.

By coincidence, during the week of Genette's disappearance, Bob Cracknell was on holiday with his family at a remote campsite not far from the Wilson home on the Cornish coast. The clairvoyant was out of normal day-to-day touch, without phone or newspapers, and claims he knew nothing of the girl's disappearance 100 miles north of him. But then he phoned Colin Wilson to say hello and was told all about it.

Immediately, Cracknell said that Genette was dead; also, that a blue car was involved. Colin Wilson was sufficiently impressed to phone a reporter he knew and suggest the BBC carry a story on these impressions.

According to both Cracknell and Wilson, the police heard the interview and were sufficiently impressed that they invited both of them to drive to Aylesbeare and assist. Wilson was interested in the case not only because of his fascination with crime, but also because by some coincidence Genette had several years before visited his house when the Tates had lived in the same small village.

Cracknell called to collect Colin Wilson on his way north and they took a day out to visit the scene of the mystery. One of the detectives involved, Donald Crabb, showed them Genette's bicycle, then took them to the Within Lane area and let the psychic describe his feelings.

He was very specific. The one thing about Bob Cracknell is that he is never afraid to be precise. He is wrong as often as he is right, but he is rarely vague.

In this case he affirmed that Genette was dead. A man had seen her when she collected the papers from outside the village pub. He had waited for her in Within Lane with the intention of a sexual assault, attracted her attention by calling her name (which he read from her T-shirt) and knocked her off the bike with a blow to the head. But he had been interrupted by Genette's two friends wandering up. So he hid in the grass beside the road with an unconscious or already dead victim until the girls left to push the bicycle away. Then he had carried the teenager across fields to his car, parked some distance away, and taken Genette to an area called Broad Oak. Detective Crabb checked and found there was such a place, a tract of common land with several boggy marshes just a couple of miles away. Cracknell insisted he had never heard of it, but the body had been put there under water. The large expanse of common was searched, of course. Nothing was found.

After being impressed by this, Crabb suggested that Cracknell and Wilson visit the Tate house. The reason the psychic took Violet away on her own was, he says, because he immediately sensed awful tension in the family focused on John Tate. Violet admitted this was so and agreed with Bob Cracknell's feeling that there had been a row on the day of the tragedy. Genette had been upset by all this.

Later, when the truth of John Tate's former difficulty was admitted, it emerged that Genette had once interrupted her father and half-sister whilst they were together, and so was aware of what was going on. That certainly suggests that Bob Cracknell's impressions in August 1978 were at least partially accurate, even though he could not have known the truth about the Tate family's past – it was two years before news of this was made public.

Colin Wilson also says that far from being upset and worn out by Bob Cracknell's visit, as John Tate reports, Genette's father stayed chatting with the author. His ex-wife Sheila, who had come down from Bristol to help in the search for her daughter, was also present.

It is obvious that Bob Cracknell failed to solve the case. He also made statements which proved to be erroneous, such as telling Detective Crabb that the murderer would be identified within ten days. Yet, if he and Wilson are presenting an accurate picture of the events of Friday 25 August 1978, it seems that outright dismissal of these psychics might be a little harsh. They may have had some value.

Yet John Alderson told us, 'The mediums were of no assistance. We couldn't find a body, if there was a body. We literally did everything orthodox and unorthodox. . . But they all drew a blank.'

The public relations officer, Roger Busby, was more specific. 'The assistance we had from these people was very interesting, but inconclusive, Cracknell was adamant we would have somebody in custody within the week. When we didn't we never heard from him again!'

However, Busby was rather more impressed by Professor Gerard Croiset, a famous Dutch psychic. His reputation has come under serious attack since his death in 1981, something we will look at more fully later on. However, because of his alleged successes in Holland, one enterprising journalist, aware of his claims to have found many bodies in similar missing person cases, requested his help. Croiset gave this without leaving his home city of Utrecht. He took a map of the Aylesbeare area and dangled a pendulum over it, getting feelings and pictures in his mind. He also immediately said that Genette had been murdered. He too said she had been placed beneath water.

Some while after this the *Daily Express* flew Croiset over to try to solve the case. He spent two days on the scene and, according to Roger Busby, 'He was able to describe without prompting the locations where Genette delivered her newspapers. But at the end of the day the psychic said, "I get this information, but I don't know if it's from the past, present or future. And if I say to the right or left then it might be the opposite because I do sometimes get a mirror image."' However, Busby concluded, 'That man obviously could detect something from the environment.'

But overall Busby was disappointed. 'It was all fascinating but vague. The psychics made statements like, "She's in a car boot", but when you ask for a registration number they say, "Sorry – I can't do that." In fact Roger Busby was very candid about exactly *why* this utilization of psychics took place. It was not with any misguided belief that they would find Genette. 'It was an unusual case because the location was so suspicious ... the classic mystery element attracted investigators into the paranormal right away ... Normally we don't deal with people like this, but it was important to us to keep the story newsworthy and in the headlines and the psychics and paranormal sources helped us to do that.'

After the police removed their incident room from Aylesbeare village and were inevitably forced to reduce the status of the enquiry because of other pressing cases, an attempt was made to set up a new 'psychic incident room'. The mastermind behind this was retired detective Dick Lee, who had been involved in the famous 'Operation Julie' drug ring coup. There was also a TV producer, Andrew Wilson, and the writer Colin Wilson, who became their 'adviser' on paranormal matters. The basic idea seems to have been to prove that whilst the police had failed badly, the psychics could succeed.

For several months this most unusual team collated dreams, images and all sorts of impressions from professional psychics and ordinary people. They scrounged help from the army and the police where they could, and even secured the co-operation of a local businessman who lent them a helicopter so that Colin Wilson could do aerial reconnaissance of likely spots. These were areas where psychics such as Bob Cracknell had pinpointed Genette's grave. Most of the mediums now believed that the murderer had returned to collect Genette's body from the marsh and moved it to somewhere less likely to be discovered.

However, the entire operation was a failure, as Colin Wilson freely admits. 'It was all a waste of time. By Christmas, when the psychic incident room closed and the team split up, we still knew no more about Genette's disappearance than on the first day of the search.' (Wilson, *The Psychic Detectives*.)

Roger Busby was less than charitable about what he saw as an attempt to demonstrate police incompetence. 'We were not very happy about them. But they still got nowhere, despite all their claims. They also couldn't find anything wrong with the police investigation!'

Whilst this mixed bunch of 'psychic detectives' was inspired by a story-hungry Thames TV in London, they were not the only media source trying to discover a new angle. The BBC current affairs programme *Tonight* also had a go.

One of the few scraps of conventional evidence that seemed valuable came from an off-duty policewoman, Mathilda Rogers, and her daughter Gail. They had actually passed Genette on Within Lane some minutes before she met and talked to her school chums. However, unlike the girls, they recalled seeing a car pass by. Unfortunately, their description of this vehicle was very limited.

Enter the BBC with the idea of conducting an on-screen experiment. Hypnosis was used to regress both witnesses back to that afternoon, in the hope that they would relive the memory sufficiently well to provide new details. Again it seemed to be a great success. Mrs Rogers and her daughter did remember a lot of extra information about the car. It was a maroon-coloured Ford Cortina, an extremely popular model at the time. However, more helpfully, a partial registration number was retrieved.

As Chief Constable John Alderson told us, 'We had almost every maroon Ford Cortina ever made traced and investigated. But this was all without result. We were advised that the subconscious mind can store information on so many things, so many cars, that we were left not knowing if this memory from hypnosis was helpful or misleading.'

Roger Busby was more disturbed. He claimed, 'The hypnosis on the police officer and her daughter was completely inconclusive . . . but the TV exaggerated and hardened it out so that the programme looked more dramatic and more conclusive.'

With a seemingly insoluble mystery such as this the temptation for police, public and media to try anything to resolve it must have been enormous. It would be a feather in anybody's cap if they could finally demonstrate what did happen to this girl.

However, another aspect to this extraordinary affair seems rather more difficult to comprehend. Because speculation about a remarkable supernatural cause for Genette's disappearance began very quickly. At face value that looks absurd because there are several all too natural, if tragic, scenarios that one could readily adopt to explain what took place. The quick way in which the teenager's vanishing trick was blamed on extraterrestrials in flying saucers is perhaps largely a testament to the human liking for the strange and unusual. It certainly seems difficult to equate with the facts.

That it was mooted was not entirely the fault of the media, but it is true that the press tended to regard such speculation as one more way to keep this tale in the forefront of attention.

This had been quite a year for UFOs. In fact there had been a major wave of sightings in 1977, followed by the premiere of the Spielberg UFO movie *Close Encounters of the Third Kind* in March 1978. So the subject was one attracting popular attention at the time. Because Margaret Heavey and Tracey Pratt had read of a sighting in the local paper the week before the terrible events of that August Saturday, it is not too surprising that they should wonder if their friend had been taken off in a 'spaceship'. After all, it is almost inevitable that we put the blame for the seemingly inexplicable upon an unknown . . . and preferably an unknown that is currently in fashion. As you will have seen from several other 1978 cases in this book, thanks largely to the Spielberg movie UFOs again certainly fitted the bill.

Indeed, if you found a friend disappearing without sight or sound, virtually right under your nose, perhaps even you might briefly wonder if some other-worldly power had designs upon her.

We have checked the records of the British UFO Research Association (BUFORA), which actually lists over 600 UK sightings for 1978. None are listed from Devon or Cornwall within several days on either side of 19 August. The only ones reported during that 24-hour spell come from Kent and the village of Hungerford in Berkshire.

The sightings which the two girls must have read about were reported from all over Britain on 14 and 15 August, and were identified by the investigators of BUFORA as bright meteors burning up high in the atmosphere. There is, in fact, an annual shower of these dust particles and rocks which brings many UFO sightings in mid-August.

Of course, such information was generally not of interest to the media. The last thing that is required in a situation like this is an explanation. That instantly defuses the story. Far better, the theory goes, to retain an air of mystery. The suggestion, however vague, that Genette Tate might be alive and well and living on Venus was too grand an illusion to puncture with just a few awkward facts.

According to debunker Melvyn Harris, this myth was foisted on to the public by UFO investigators. He says, 'Needless to say the Genette Tate case is still unresolved and if the ufologists are to be believed, it will stay that way. They maintain she was kidnapped by a Venusian space craft . . .'

Well, we tried rather hard to find any ufologist who endeavoured to convince anyone of this. We could not. BUFORA had actually resolved the question of those lights in the sky over the West Country on their own initiative, and very quickly. There is no sign that they ever claimed them to be UFOs from Venus or anywhere else.

However, there is no doubt that once the idea was trotted out by the press, based initially on the speculations of Genette Tate's friends, it was not very hard for the local media to find know-it-all, self-professed 'experts' on everything . . . including UFOs. They were not, so far as we can tell, UFO researchers. But the problem with most aspects of the supernatural is that you need no qualifications to call yourself a 'ufologist' or 'ghostbuster'. In the days of rising unemployment it became something of a fad to adopt this title after reading a few books. It may enhance someone's standing in the community, but prepared them for little, other than making an ass of themselves.

One thing turned this case on its head so far as the UFO theory is concerned. Someone, nobody seems to know who, chanced to remark that a crescent-shaped patch in a field, close to the spot on Within Lane where Genette had vanished, *might* have been created by 'exhaust' from a 'spaceship'. It probably started as a joke. But that sort of claim is like gold dust to an eager reporter and the story was, of course, heavily promoted. In this way the completely groundless idea of a UFO kidnap was given a degree of superficial plausibility.

In fact, as Roger Busby explained to us, 'Nobody would listen to the truth, which was that this mark had simply resulted from the farmer who owned the field putting too much lime on it by mistake.'

Another theory bit the dust. But police chief John Alderson acknowledged that it may never die in the public imagination. 'The idea of flying saucers was discussed during our police enquiries. There may be some kind of extraterrestrial body involved on earth, who can positively argue otherwise? Even today there are still people who genuinely think like that. Some have speculated that this is how Genette disappeared, and really who can say?'

We heard murmurings during our investigation of this sad case that the former Chief Constable was a little too soft on the paranormal and somewhat gullible in terms of his willingness to entertain bizarre ideas. We also heard it alleged that his influence was the main reason why Genette's disappearance became so heavily associated with supernatural trappings. You must reach your own conclusions from the quotes that we offer.

We found John Alderson refreshingly open-minded. We could certainly see no evidence that his brave decision to give credence to the *possibility* of unconventional methods or explanations (and that is quite different from accepting them as proven fact) in any way compromised the police investigation of this case. Indeed, it may well be argued with some force that, by broadening the scope of enquiries in what was frankly an impossible investigation, at least some hope of a breakthrough was retained when otherwise there was none.

John Alderson was very forthright when we put this to him.

'My personal view is that if a police force cannot solve a mystery and some people say they can, even if they may seem a little odd, you have a moral responsibility to let them try. But you have to be careful with what facts you give them access to. And you must have anything they tell you corroborated by *real* clues. It might start you on a line of enquiry. That's about the best that you can hope for.'

Of course, we have not solved the mystery of Genette Tate's disappearance. The purpose of this discussion was to examine the way in which the supernatural played a major role in other people's efforts to find a resolution. However, it is perhaps appropriate to close by allowing the two major police spokesmen to tell us what they believe.

Roger Busby is fairly restrained. 'The most likely theory is that she was abducted by someone who had the luck of the devil and got out of the area without being seen.'

As for John Alderson, he obviously feels deeply about this matter. 'There are dozens of cases that are never brought to court because you don't have the evidence. But you do have clues. Here we don't have any. It's amazing. This was the most frustrating and galling case I have ever been involved with. This is a true mystery . . . All we know is the time she was last seen and that she was around the corner alive and well. Of course, obviously something happened to the girl. But we still don't know if she is alive or dead.

'It was a very dispiriting case. We are almost as far from a solution today as we were then . . . If you are not careful you can let your imagination lead you all over the place when it is such a mystery. But as a policeman that is not good. You have to deal in facts . . . Perhaps one day someone will make a deathbed confession, if the girl is dead somewhere. But otherwise we may never know any more than we do now.'

Crime and the Supernatural . . .
A Summing Up

Throughout this book we have attempted not to take sides on the reality or otherwise of paranormal phenomena. To a large extent this is not what we are presently concerned with. This book is really about how and why the world of the supernatural is used in the context of crime or sudden death.

You must assess the individual stories in their own right and decide for yourself whether, for example, Frederick Valentich engineered his own disappearance, died thanks to the intervention of human hands, or might really be residing on some other world right now.

Similarly, you might question the guilt or innocence of Carol Compton, and your conclusion could depend upon how willing you are to accept the existence of a phenomenon that most scientists have not accepted. Frankly, their scepticism does not make them right, or you wrong. Science is all about learning new things, and one prediction we can make without any ESP is that in fifty years' time schoolkids will know about things that no scientist on earth believes in today. That was once true of atomic radiation, radio waves, laser beams and computers. It will be true of other things in the future, and some of them might be what we now choose to label as supernatural or paranormal.

What today is paranormal may tomorrow be quite mundane. But that is not a rule without exception. If it were then we would still be divining entrails and using leeches to treat serious medical conditions. Some beliefs *are* superstitions and history will fail to vindicate them.

Both these factors must be borne in mind when contemplating the cases that we reviewed. However, we were much more interested in how these stories came to be associated with strange phenomena. The responsibility can be shouldered by many people. Of course, it is true that newspapers often tell the tale in huge banner headlines, perhaps with scant regard for the facts. But the media on the whole simply reflect human interest and the cultural mood of the times. There has undoubtedly been in recent years a rebellion against science which has sought to explain *everything* in materialistic terms, from the building blocks of matter to the nature of God.

Materialism went too far. Some scientists now realize this, and there is a curious reversal which is seeing many research workers encompassing ideas such as that of 'a creator' in their mathematical theorems. But whilst the rebellion may have an identifiable cause, that does not mean it was a wholly glorious revolution. It, too, has reached extremes.

There are dangers inherent in allowing astrological predictions in every newspaper or magazine to dictate one's life, to whatever extent. Not even the most ardent proponents of the supernatural believe there is any sense in that. And this is but an illustration of the manner in which our desire to have mystery and wonder in our lives has blinkered our thinking in many subtle ways.

True open-mindedness is a willingness to believe that something may be right or may be wrong. Too many people have set themselves up on opposite sides of a great divide, and have become so firmly stuck to one set of beliefs or another that they are unable to analyse any situation with proper clarity.

Believing that when a person bursts into flames in a frighteningly sudden manner it *must* be as a result of some mysterious force known as 'spontaneous human combustion' is just as untenable as instructing a jury to dismiss all thought of this possibility from their minds.

The world needs more tolerance towards ideas about the paranormal. But it also needs less wild exuberance in their support. The majority of occurrences which *look* supernatural will almost certainly have simple and quite rational explanations. But some might not. To recognize this fact needs a reappraisal from the believers as well as from the sceptics. And until that happens we will continue to find the subject abused, raised to new heights of absurdity, and denied its proper place in the scheme of things.

Every one of the cases described in this book deserves serious consideration. They should be debated by the media and the public, subjected to enquiries, and examined in the same way that we might discuss other major topical issues. Without the supernatural trimmings they would probably earn this respect. Because of the ballyhoo, they are relegated to pamphlets in occult bookshops, and bar-room jokes. That must be overcome. This simple fact is the main reason why we undertook this book.

Perhaps the one area where crime and the supernatural are coming into even closer contact is that touched on in our last case, the tragic disappearance of Genette Tate. For on an increasing scale so-called 'psychic detectives' are being called in to assist police forces.

This is a typical case from the USA, reported by researcher Lawrence Cortesi. It occurred in the late seventies in New York State, following a series of brutal murders in and around Schenectady and Albany.

The local police had no answers to the double death of religious art shop owner Robert Hedderman and his assistant Margaret Bryon, found in a pool of blood on 26 November 1976. Lieutenant Edward Jones attempted to secure psychic help, but his superior, assistant police chief William Van Arnam, reacted to Jones's suggestion that Albany clairvoyant Ann Fisher be consulted with the comment that he could do it, but 'You are on your own.'

Jones took Ann Fisher to the scene of the crime (the now disused shop) in the belief that whatever emerged he could not end up with fewer clues than he already had. But Ann Fisher was horrified at the 'bad vibes' she instantly sensed inside the still bloodstained building. She felt that the killer was 'a pathological murderer who would surely kill again if the police did not catch him'.

Lieutenant William Murray, another of the detectives present that day, said the psychic looked like a 'zombie' as she walked out into the frozen streets of the town in a virtual trance. But she gave a specific description of the big black man aged about forty whom she said was responsible. Moreover, she went around the back to an alley and pointed out a dumper inside which was found a piece of cloth covered in blood that all prior searches had missed. It later proved to have been used by the killer to wipe his bloodied hands. Then she described the place where the killer worked, which matched a building very near the scene. Routine enquiries revealed that a man fitting Ann Fisher's description had recently worked there.

Lieutenant Murray likened the clairvoyant to 'a hound following a psychic scent'. But the police felt that no jury would convict the man on psychic evidence. Besides, Ann Fisher was sure that if her role in the matter emerged the killer would attack her to ensure silence!

The man was only caught a year later following another murder, although he had been watched carefully for that period. The bloodstained cloth, along with the evidence appertaining to the second tragedy, secured his conviction. The sad thing is that, but for the stigma of 'psychic detection', it is possible that the second murder could have been prevented.

Coincidence? Or do we accept the verdict of the police officers that this case might never have been solved but for the psychic providing them with real evidence?

This kind of thing is by no means new. Journalist and paranormal researcher Alan Cleaver gave us details of a case in the Thame area of the Oxfordshire/Buckinghamshire border.

William Edden had died at the hands of an unknown assailant near the village of Haddenham as he walked home from a visit to the market. Back in Thame, his wife had a vision of the crime at the time of her husband's death and told disbelieving friends and neighbours what had happened. When the authorities began an enquiry into the matter, startled by her intimate knowledge of the tragedy, she shocked them further by naming Benjamin Tyler as the murderer.

Tyler denied the charge and, again, no action could be taken on evidence as flimsy as a 'vision'. But a year later, labourer Solomon Sewell confessed that he had witnessed the act and Tyler had done it. Tyler's defence was that Sewell was a simpleton; even the youth's mother supported Tyler in that regard. The labourer's testimony was thrown out as unreliable.

But a year later, with Mrs Edden still insisting that her husband's ghost had appeared at the time of his death and pointed out Tyler as the killer, another trial occurred. This time both Benjamin Tyler and Solomon Sewell were charged with the crime, and, largely on the evidence of Mrs Edden's vision, were found guilty and hanged. Tyler protested his innocence even on the scaffold.

This crime and psychic detection took place in 1828.

Naturally, we are faced with serious questions here. If criminals are being brought to justice even partially on the evidence of psychic visions, we need to know more about the accuracy of such things. The example of Genette Tate was not awfully encouraging although Gerard Croiset was highly praised. Yet, as pointed out at the time, Croiset has had his detractors.

Sceptical researcher Piet Hein Hoebens was particularly interested in why such a small country as Holland should produce three world-renowned psychic detectives, of whom Croiset was one. On the face of things it does seem odd.

In a series of in-depth reports for *Zetetic Scholar* (a magazine edited by sociologist Dr Marcello Truzzi at Eastern Michigan University, and one of the few truly objective publications on such matters) Hoebens made extensive enquiries into the past of three of the Dutch 'paragnosts', as they are locally named.

In Issue 8 (1981) his target was Peter van der Hurk (who moved to the USA, renamed himself Peter Hurkos and became one of the most famous clairvoyants of the twentieth century). Hurkos had supposedly gained his powers in 1941 when he fell off a ladder, and then used his abilities to help the Allied resistance. But each of the reported stories Hoebens checked into either was exaggerated beyond all recognition or had no substance, in his opinion.

His research into Gerard Croiset was published in Issue 9 (1982) and was equally disturbing. Whilst Hoebens agreed that he had much credibility in Holland, and Croiset was 'a genuine challenge to the skeptic', he nonetheless found problems. In several cases that he looked into Croiset publicly claimed that he had given highly specific information about a missing child, for example. In fact, it transpired that he had only confirmed existing suspicions or used logical deductive methods.

For instance, in one case from 1951, a seven-year-old child was missing. The story goes that Croiset told Utrecht police he was dead and would be found under water (interestingly this is virtually identical to his prognosis on Genette Tate twenty-seven years later). The boy was found just as the psychic had said. However, it is the omission of information which is important here. Croiset failed to explain that he knew the family, had initially told them all would be well, and only after a canal right beside where the child lived had been searched for several days did his 'dead under water' prediction appear. This hardly required paranormal powers to guess at that stage.

In other words, it does seem sensible that we be cautious about how willingly we accept the stories of psychic detectives. Despite Croiset claiming that he was part of a 'team' which Dutch police used regularly, Hoebens found no such thing. Every former senior police officer he talked to was critical and sceptical. As our experience showed with the Devon and Cornwall police, this is not inevitable, if results seem to justify acclaim. But this lukewarm response to Croiset does suggest that the reputation of a psychic can be touched up a little for public consumption.

Croiset was one of those involved in perhaps the most extensive 'psychic investigation' of all time. This was the hunt for a mass murderer, the so-called Yorkshire Ripper.

The killings began at Keighley, West Yorkshire, in July 1975 and spanned over five years and thirteen brutal slayings in Yorkshire and Lancashire. During this time one major clue was a tape recording and several letters sent by the man whom the police believed to be the murderer, who introduced himself with the words 'I'm Jack' (a deliberate reference to his 'Jack the Ripper' reputation). The accent was clearly that of a Northeast man and this ensured that the focus of all enquiries was directed in this area.

That proved to be a catastrophic error. The letters and tape were a hoax and had not been sent by the killer at all, but a man still at large who had decided to play games with the publicity. Forensic evidence later proved that beyond any reasonable doubt.

However, just as the tape led the police and the British media into the false belief that the killer was a Geordie, it also seems to have misled the psychics who were frequently used by the press (if not the police) to give new leads on this crime story of the century.

The famous medium Doris Stokes, whose reputation must rank alongside Uri Geller in terms of both fame and fortune, gave a front-page story to the *Sunday People* on 1 July 1979. She insisted she had seen the Ripper in a vision and described him to an artist, who shocked the nation with an 'identikit' portrait for the newspaper. The murderer was clean-shaven, with a scar on his cheek, one of his eyes twitched, and he lived in the Sunderland area. His name was Ronnie or Johnnie, Doris insisted. A lot of other very precise information was given to Doris by the killer's dead mother, she said.

This caused considerable embarrassment to long-distance lorry driver Ronnie Metcalf, from Sunderland, who fitted the description very well and even lived in a road with a similar name to the one Doris Stokes had offered the journalists. Metcalf voluntarily came forward to explain how he was now being harassed by people who took the psychic at her word and believed he must be the killer.

Shortly afterwards the *Sun* turned to Gerard Croiset for their own portrait of the murderer. Croiset gave an account very similar to that of Doris Stokes, which he should have known about. He too insisted the killer had long straight hair and lived in some flats in Sunderland. He even picked out the correct block of flats from an aerial photograph!

When the Ripper was finally caught in January 1981, he turned out to be a man that police had previously interviewed, but mistakenly released, partly thanks to all the misleading suspicions about the Northeast which the psychics had helped to foster.

The real Ripper looked nothing like the descriptions of either Doris Stokes or Gerard Croiset and certainly did not have any connection with Sunderland. None of the other details given by these extraordinary detectives were accurate.

Of course, both might argue that the man they *did* see is

the one still at large, who faked the letters and tapes and pretended to be the Ripper. If so, the police can only say that the clues of the psychic detectives were checked out and, specific as they were, they all proved of no help in finding the man whose false evidence contributed directly to the wrong trail the investigation took and indirectly to the death of several later victims of the killer.

Nevertheless, there was one amazing series of clues offered by clairvoyant Nella Jones. These were given to freelance journalist Shirley Davenport between October 1979 and November 1980, when she was working on the psychic's autobiography, *A Ghost of a Chance*.

Jenny Randles met Ms Davenport soon after the Yorkshire Ripper was captured and the writer confirmed the substance of what Nella Jones had told her. For example, the medium had said the killer was called Peter and he was a long-distance lorry driver (as, rather interestingly, was the man Doris Stokes had innocently fingered). However, unlike all the other psychics, Nella had insisted that Peter did *not* come from the Northeast but lived in an elevated house, numbered 6, in Bradford, West Yorkshire. She added other details; for example, that his truck bore the name of the company he worked for on the cab door and it began with the letter 'C'. The killer was also due to strike again on 17 November 1980, she told Shirley Davenport a few days beforehand.

We are to some extent reliant upon the word of the psychic and her scribe. But we have found no reason to doubt either. And Nella Jones was amazingly accurate, because almost every one of the details she gave proved correct. The Ripper *was* a lorry driver and his cab door *did* bear the name of the firm he worked for (Clark Holdings). His name *was* Peter and he lived at 6 Garden Lane, an elevated house in Bradford, West Yorkshire.

Peter Sutcliffe (I think we must point out *not* the same Peter Sutcliffe who is a key witness in the case of Yorkshire miner Zigmund Adamski) murdered his last victim in Leeds on the exact day in November 1980 that Nella Jones allegedly predicted.

Of course, the dilemma all this presents for the police is quite significant. The facts show that nearly all well-publicized crimes generate offers of psychic assistance. Even those from the most celebrated clairvoyants, and so the ones who achieve most publicity and seem on the surface to be the most likely to offer real clues, can be way off-beam and entirely wrong. Yet, lurking within the mass of testimony, there might be some information from a psychic which is astonishingly accurate. How do you tell the difference between the good, the bad and the plain misleading? And is the result more confusion rather than positive assistance?

Perhaps the police would stand a better chance on a less highly publicized case, where only genuinely motivated local psychics would come forward to offer their help.

We spoke to one man who has had experience of this field. His name is Dr John Dale, a clinical psychologist from Stockport, Cheshire. During the day he earns his living treating patients with phobias and neuroses. In his spare time he sometimes assists British police forces with his extraordinary talent for psychometry.

A psychometrist claims to be able to hold an object and 'read' emotions that cling to it. These emotions supposedly come from the person who last owned or used it. If it is something that played a part in a crime, for example a murder weapon, then theoretically, Dr Dale believes, he could pick up information about the killer. This would come in the form of pictures in his mind's eye; dramatizations in the form of day dreams. They would be based on the factual data picked up, but as he said, 'The problems start with the act of translation. I am receiving emotions and feelings and these are being turned into pictures in my head. I can be wrong just as often as I am right. And when I am wrong, then I am certainly wrong!'

Dr Dale showed Jenny Randles details of several cases where he has assisted the police, usually in missing persons enquiries similar to that of Genette Tate. He satisfied us as to the veracity of this work, but explained, 'The details are confidential. I do not do this for publicity and only when asked. I do not go to the police and ask them if I can help. Normally they prefer not to make public that they have received my kind of assistance and would probably not report that I did help them, but privately they have often thanked me – even in writing – for what I have done.'

In May 1986 John Dale allowed Jenny Randles to conduct some experiments with a BBC radio producer as part of a series of documentaries she was making. He certainly provided several bits of information simply from handling a piece of jewellery that belonged to the woman ... although he had no idea who this was and Jenny was herself totally ignorant of the personal circumstances of the owner until after the experiment. But, just as Dr Dale had warned, there were as many spectacular goofs as there were successes.

The psychologist does not profess to be a psychic. He believes that he has simply trained himself to use a skill that everyone possesses. 'I made a study of psychics when I was training. I concluded that if these people are not born biologically different from the rest of us, then there was no reason why I should not be able to do what they claimed they could do.'

However, he approaches his work with refreshing objectivity, and is well aware of the dangers of over-credulity. 'It is so easy to let your own beliefs creep in. It's not a case of "seeing is believing". It's really more that what you believe in is ultimately what you are going to see.'

It is interesting to speculate how this might apply to psychic intervention in another on-going case, the police search for further victims of Moors Murderers Myra Hindley and Ian Brady. Throughout 1987 there were searches of the Pennine hills around Saddleworth on the Yorkshire/Lancashire border, as several of their victims were said to be buried there.

Fresh digging had been productive, but for most of 1987 the object of the search was to trace the grave of twelve-year-old Keith Bennett, who vanished from his home in Longsight, Manchester, in 1965. Hindley and Brady have admitted that they killed him and buried him on the moors, but his body remained undiscovered.

On 28 July 1987 psychic detective Stephen Alexander issued a press statement that a breakthrough was imminent. He alleged that police had involved him in the case from 1966, when he was only nineteen! Now he had seen a vision of the discovery of Bennett's grave. Ian Brady, he said, would be flown to Saddleworth moors by helicopter from the top security hospital on Merseyside where he has spent many years. This would enable Greater Manchester police to pinpoint the grave of the boy, which would be in the Shiny Brook area in a place where a tiny stream in a hollow was surrounded by many rocks that look like a star when viewed from a certain angle. The boy's remains would be found just feet away, but only sometime after Brady had been flown back to Liverpool. All of this was going to happen within five weeks of Alexander's July statement.

There had been much speculation for months beforehand about Brady following in the footsteps of Myra Hindley (who had already been to the moors to guide new police enquiries). However, the psychic's timing was way off, even if his reasonable speculation about the killer's trip was eventually proved accurate.

Ian Brady *was* taken back to the moors in December 1987, more than four months (not five weeks) after Alexander's 'vision'. He was taken by van and not by helicopter. But he *did* centre the resurrected police search on the Shiny Brook area, although this was no surprise as it was where most people thought the body would be. As we write, it remains to be seen whether the psychic proves correct and Keith Bennett's grave is found under the circumstances he predicted. But that Stephen Alexander was proved wrong on some points demonstrates the truth of John Dale's warnings.

It might be appropriate to end with one more cautionary tale that perhaps summarizes the problems and the risks of interweaving the supernatural with tragic deaths.

On 15 December 1980, 31-year-old nurse Melanie Uribe disappeared as she drove to work in a hilly area of California, part of the vast suburban sprawl that is Los Angeles. There were immediate fears for her safety as a young girl's body had recently been discovered in the same area.

The story was of course soon spread around the neighbourhood, and 32-year-old Etta Smith, who worked in the offices of the Lockheed Aircraft Corporation, learnt about it on the night of the 16th from a friend who worked in the nursing profession.

At 3 P.M. the next day, 17 December, the story broke publicly on the radio. As soon as Etta Smith heard the broadcast she was overcome by a strange feeling and 'knew' that the nurse was lying dead in a canyon. She had a vivid mental impression of what the area looked like. Despite her qualms, she drove to the police station involved in the hunt on her way home from work. Here she told her unlikely story to detective Lee Ryan, who requested that she pinpoint the spot on a map. She did so, and seemed to feel that Lopez Canyon was the place. The police took her name and address and promised to look into the matter, although one wonders how serious their intention was.

Back at home the matter weighed heavily on Mrs Smith's mind. Visions like this were not routine for her; even though she had undergone a few minor telepathic experiences beforehand. When she told her two young children, they were caught up in the excitement and wanted to go to Lopez Canyon right away to see if they could find the body.

They all drove there and, just before fear got the better of them, spotted something white in the dust. Getting out of the car they walked towards it, before panicking and running back. On the way out of the canyon they met a police patrol. Etta Smith stopped it and led the driver back to where the body of Melanie Uribe did indeed lie.

Within an hour of arriving back home, Etta Smith discovered that the nightmare she believed to be over was in fact just about to begin. The police arrived and took her back for 'routine questioning'. It soon became clear that they were not happy with her story and were 'disturbed' that she had 'seen' the girl wearing the correct clothing, which was different from what one might expect a nurse to be wearing, and, of course, by the way she had found the spot where the body lay purely on the strength of a vision.

They asked if Etta Smith would take a polygraph test. Despite by now being tired, hungry and scared she agreed. It was the early hours of the morning and the lie detector operator advised that the test be postponed or repeated later. But Etta wanted to get back home to her family. She took the test. It was inconclusive.

Now the police became increasingly aggressive. They told her that they were intending to arrest her for murder!

Mrs Smith was not charged, but she was kept in a police cell for four days whilst a decision was reached on what to do. In the meantime, police had discovered that the nurse had been attacked by three men who had jumped her pickup when it was stationary at traffic lights. The men had raped her and killed her with a rock. These men were later arrested and convicted of the crime.

In March 1987 Etta took her case against the police to the Los Angeles courts. Evidence on her behalf was given by several sources, including the polygraph operator and detective Lee Ryan, to whom she first reported her vision. According to journalist Richard Varenchik, who was present, Ryan called her arrest 'a miscarriage of justice'.

Etta Smith's lawyer demanded $750,000 in damages when the court found in her favour. In the end the jury agreed on a much lower sum of $26,184 (about £15,000).

In view of the dramatic increase in the interaction between the police and psychic detectives this case might not be the last of its kind. It is perhaps rather fortunate that most visions turn out to be vague and at least partially inaccurate. For if they were more precise, our jails might soon be full of some very unusual and most unlucky inmates.

Acknowledgments

Newspaper accounts reported include:

'Secret file on UFO invasion'; *Warrington Guardian*, 17 March 1978

Genette Tate reports in the *Guardian*, 25 August 1978

'May the force be with you'; *Hebden Bridge Times*, 5 December 1980

'Local bobby's close encounter intrigues the world'; *Hebden Bridge Times*, 4 December 1981

John Sheard and Stewart Bonney, articles in the *Sunday Mirror* on 27 September 1981 ('Amazing UFO Death Riddle') and 29 November 1981 ('The alien terror of PC Godfrey')

'College in quiz over girl who died in flames'; *Daily Express*, 25 February 1985

'Inquest quashes fire death rumours'; *Widnes Weekly News*, week of 1 July 1985

Bolton triangle reported in *Bolton Evening News*, 6 June 1987

Magazines referred to include:

ASSAP News 65 Amersham Rd, High Wycombe, Bucks HP13 5AA, England

BUFORA 16 South Way, Burgess Hill, Sussex RH15 9ST, England

Fate (see Lawrence Cortesi in July 1987, 448; Richard Varenchik, August 1987, 449) 3510 Western Avenue, Highland Park, Ill. 60035, USA

Fortean Times 96 Mansfield Road, London NW3 2HX, England
FSR Snodland, Kent ME6 5HJ, England
MUFON 103 Oldtowne Rd, Seguine, Texas 78155, USA
Stigmata PO Box 1094, Paris, Texas 75460, USA
Zetetic Scholar Dept of Sociology, Eastern Michigan University, Ypsilanti, Michigan 48159, USA

Books referred to in the text include:

Clues to the Unknown, Robert Cracknell, Hamlyn, 1981
The Kaikoura UFOs, Bill Startup and Bob Guard, Hodder, 1981
Let's Hope They're Friendly, Quentin Fogarty, Angus & Robertson, 1982
The Pennine UFO Mystery, Jenny Randles, Grafton, 1983
Mute Evidence, Daniel Kagan & Ian Summers, Bantam, 1984
Genette: Where Is She Now?, John Tate, Lion, 1985
Sorry You've Been Duped, Melvyn Harris, Weidenfeld & Nicolson, 1986
The Hidden Power, Brian Inglis, Chatto, 1987
Modern Mysteries of Britain, Janet & Colin Bord, Grafton, 1987
Arthur C. Clarke's Chronicles of the Strange and Mysterious, Simon Welfare & John Fairley, Collins, 1987
The UFO Conspiracy, Jenny Randles, Javelin, 1988

People to whom special thanks are owed include:

John Alderson, Larry Arnold, Michael Burt, Roger Busby, Ian Cameron, Bill Chalker, Alan Cleaver, Norman Collinson, Barbara Edwards, Alan Godfrey, Sandy Gregg, Dr Richard Haines, Harry Harris, Roy Kirkpatrick, Richard Lawrence, Serena Macbeth, Andrew McCallum, Linda Moulton Howe, Paul Norman, Malcolm Robinson, Mike Sacks, Bob Thomson.